Young Muslim Voices

Copyright © 2022 by Mafiq Foundation, Inc.

All rights reserved. No part of this publication may be reproduced, stored in a retrieved system, transmitted or utilized, in any form or by any means, electronic, mechanical, photocopying, recording or otherwise, without the prior permission of the publisher.

Printed in the United States of America

Published by:
Mafiq foundation, Inc
P. O. Box 730
Herndon VA 20172 USA
E-mail: essays@mafiq.org
Website: https://mafiq.org

CONTENTS

Dedication v
Quranic Verses and Hadiths vi
Committee Information viii
Foreword ix
Preface xi
Reflections on the Judging Process xii
Introduction xiv

2020 Essays: The Prophet of Peace and Justice............... 1
- Elementary School- Level 1 3
- Elementary School- Level 2 13
- Middle School- Level 3 27
- Middle School- Level 4 39
- High School- Level 5 53
- High School- Level 6 61

2021 Essays: Navigating the COVID-19 Pandemic........... 75
- Elementary School- Level 1 77
- Elementary School- Level 2 87
- Middle School- Level 3 99
- Middle School- Level 4 113
- High School- Level 5 129
- High School- Level 6 147

2022 Essays: Islam and Mental Health 161
- Elementary School- Level 1 163
- Elementary School- Level 2 171
- Middle School- Level 3 183

- Middle School- Level 4 197
- High School- Level 6 213

Appendix A: From the EPC Community 225
Appendix B: EPC Guidelines 226
Appendix C: EPC Participant List 229
Appendix D: EPC Judges 242
Appendix E: Glossary 253

Dedicated to the Muslim community and the students, parents, and organizers that work hard to make the Essay Panel Competition (EPC) possible. May Allah (SWT) reward everyone involved immensely for all their efforts and may everyone reap the rewards of these efforts in this life and the hereafter, Ameen.

QURANIC VERSES AND HADITHS

"O you who have believed, be persistently standing firm in justice, witnesses for Allah, even if it be against yourselves or parents and relatives. Whether one is rich or poor, Allah is more worthy of both. So, follow not [personal] inclination, lest you not be just. And if you distort [your testimony] or refuse [to give it], then indeed Allah is ever, of what you do, Aware."

[Al-Quran; Surah An-Nisa 4:135]

"And cause not corruption upon the earth after its reformation. And invoke Him in fear and aspiration. Indeed, the mercy of Allah is near to the doers of good."

[Al-Quran; Surah Al-A'raf 7:56]

"O you who have believed, seek help through patience and prayer. Indeed, Allah is with the patient."

[Al-Quran; Surah Al-Baqarah 2:153]

"Wondrous is the affair of the believer, for there is good for him in every matter, and this is not the case with anyone except the believer.

If he is happy, he thanks Allah and thus there is good for him, and if he is harmed, then he shows patience and thus there is good for him."

[Sahih Muslim]

EPC Steering Committee:

Farid Ahmed, Ph. D

Zahra Ahmed, MD

Mohammad S. Choudhury, Ph. D

Mostafiz R. Chowdhury, Ph. D

Ayman Nassar, M.Sc.

Mahfuz Rahman, M.Sc.

Umaima Jafri, B. Tech

Editorial Committee:

Sidra Siddiqui, Editor

Amirah Ahmad

Doha Nassar

FOREWORD

Mafiq Foundation's Essay Panel Contest provides young Muslim students a platform to express their ideologies and perspectives surrounding issues that affect their daily lives. We are in a state of constant change, and the last three years proved especially daunting. With the rise of the Coronavirus (COVID-19), our daily routines changed, and we adapted to new social norms. Community gatherings halted, fear crept into our minds, and many loved ones were lost.

Mafiq challenged its participants to reflect on the peace and blessings that Islam provides us, a stark contrast amid the chaos of these unprecedented times. In 2020, our young Muslim voices turned to the sunnah of the Prophet (PBUH) to learn the importance of staying peaceful amid violence and chaos. In 2021, they reflected upon the hidden blessings they uncovered within the global pandemic. And in 2022, they expressed ways in which we can maintain a positive mindset amid the challenges we continue to encounter daily.

The youth wrote powerful pieces reflecting on embracing Islam's beauty and maintaining balance and wellness in our everyday lives. They share narratives of love, loss, hardship, friendship, patience, and perseverance. InshaAllah through this publication, the words of our youth can leave a lasting impact on our hearts. As you read their words and reflections, ponder on your own experiences and challenges.

May Allah (SWT) allow their words to be a source of knowledge to us all. May Allah increase them in wisdom and keep their hearts pure and full of gratitude and peace as they spread the message of Islam.

Doha Nassar
EPC Judge

PREFACE

Alhamdulillah, all praises be to Allah (SWT) for giving us the opportunity to publish another volume of the Young Muslim Voices (YMV) in the post-Covid era. Essays and letters published here are voices of the young Muslim brothers and sisters from Grade One through Twelve of Washington DC Metro and beyond. The pandemic era has opened the door for virtual participation and let us hear the voices of the youth beyond the Washington DC metro.

These writings reflect the youth's understanding, values, and intellect, giving us pleasant insight into their contribution and immense potential. Hope you enjoy the essays. Thank you for being a part of and giving the opportunity to promote and encourage youth to express their positive thoughts and improve solid communication skills.

We pray that Allah (SWT) accepts their efforts as good deeds and continues to bless them with the adornment of faith and include them among the righteously guided ones.

Mohammad Mahboob
President, Mafiq Foundation

REFLECTIONS ON THE JUDGING PROCESS

Mafiq's Essay Panel Contest (EPC) has been serving and advancing the Muslim community in the United States for almost two decades. As a former participant and now a judge, I can attest to the value of the contest in developing communication skills in Muslim youth and giving them the confidence to explore complex topics related to their identity as Muslims. EPC trains participants from different backgrounds and schools to express and articulate their thoughts in a growth-oriented platform while receiving constructive feedback. The topics chosen for the contest each year relate to moral values and pertinent social issues that the participants can relate to and apply in their lives. This year, the theme was about Islam and mental health, with a specific topic tailored to each age range.

While most participants write essays, younger participants in first and second grade write letters to a chosen recipient. This aids them in brainstorming and allows them to mentally contextualize their writing by addressing it to a familiar audience. The rest of the participants used a standard essay format to express their thoughts in an organized and cogent way. They often utilize examples from history, contemporary events, and their personal lives to illustrate their points and apply them to realistic scenarios.

Once participants submit their essays, the judges begin reading and grading them. Judges are briefed in an orientation on how to use the detailed rubric to judge essays. Each grade level is assigned approximately three judges who read, score and provide feedback on each essay. The essays are scored based on the clarity and originality of the ideas, how well the ideas are substantiated, and the quality and structure of the writing. The feedback is then sent to the participants in time for them to incorporate it into their preparation for the speech competition.

As participants prepare for the speech, they are encouraged to adapt their essays to a format more suitable for oral delivery. During the competition, participants present their speeches before a panel of judges, the other participants, and an audience of parents and community members. Judges score each speech based on a rubric that assesses both the content of the speech and the quality of the participant's delivery. This includes their eloquence and fluency in speaking, their interaction with the audience using eye contact, and their variation in tone and pitch to communicate their ideas effectively.

Although the judges determine winners based on a combined essay and speech score, the success of the participants rests more on their attentiveness to the process of brainstorming, researching, and preparing the written and oral product. EPC judges seek to further build on these skills by providing feedback and constructive criticism on participants' essays and speeches on competition day. Before and during the competition, judges spend hours working to enhance the skills of Muslim youth and prepare them to be productive and valuable members of society. Their aim is to produce young Muslims who will advance the cause of Islam in the United States, be vanguards of community service, and leaders in *da'wah* as the first line of defense for Muslims.

Amirah Ahmad
EPC Judge

INTRODUCTION

This 10th volume of Young Muslim Voices (YMV) is a compilation of three years' worth of winning essays from the Essay Panel Competition. These essays are the voice of our future generation and are a wonderful insight into how the minds of our youth work.

These are the children and young adults who will go on to become leaders and representatives of our ummah. It has been a delight to read through every single piece and look at the great minds of our youth at work. Each participant has displayed an admirable understanding of the topics and has communicated their ideas imposingly.

The entire team is grateful for this opportunity. It is heartening to see that the future of our ummah is secure in the hands of these youngsters inshaAllah.

Having started in 2002, the EPC has grown incredibly, with children and young adults participating from beyond just the DMV area. This project results from the hard work of several people- judges, volunteers, participants, parents of the participants, committee members, sponsors, and the editorial staff.

May Allah accept the efforts of everyone involved and reward them, aameen.

Introduction

EPC Program Structure

For those who may not be familiar with or may want to replicate the EPC program in their communities, below is a brief outline of how this program is structured.

First, an overall theme is determined that relates to the everyday experiences of American Muslims in the current societal context. Essay contest topics are then selected to encourage the participants to examine and ponder different Islamic subjects, thereby nudging them to hone their analytical skills and capability to express their thoughts and beliefs effectively in writing.

Each year, students from elementary school to college, split into separate levels, compete in this theme-based essay contest. This edition of the YMV book has three years of essays and, therefore, three different topics. In the first round, participants follow guidelines to put together their essays.

The elementary level focuses on a basic application of the principles of Islam and its message. The middle school level requires a deeper understanding and focuses on matters concerning morality and character. Finally, the high school level topics require reflection on and analysis of contemporary issues facing Muslim societies.

The submissions are then read, scored, and ranked by the judges. The highest scorers from this round are then moved to the next round, which is a speech competition. The winning essays and speeches are compiled and published in the Young Muslim Voices series.

The Essay Panel Competition extends beyond written and spoken essays to multimedia and poster competitions. These are the creative components of the contest, and they provide us with a glimpse of our participants' artistic abilities. Some of these posters have been included in the book.

The essays in this book result from an acute understanding, insight, and the hard work of our young participants. We hope you enjoy reading them as much as we did.

Disclaimer: The participants' essays have not been changed at all unless a spelling error had to be rectified. The only things that have been edited within the essays are the wordings of the ahadith and the Quranic verses in order to maintain uniformity throughout the book. I have followed Saheeh International's translation for the Quranic ayahs and have checked and verified every Hadith to the best of my ability.

Sidra Siddiqui
Editor

2020

The Prophet of Peace and Justice

ELEMENTARY SCHOOL | LEVEL 1

Topic:

Write a letter to your beloved one explaining what you know about being a peaceful person in Islam. Tell him/her about the lessons you have learned from Prophet (SAWS) stories in becoming a peaceful person.

This poster was submitted by Raha of level 1.

Young Muslim Voices

**1st Place: Yaaseen Ahmed
ICCL, Laurel, MD**

Dear Qasim,

Assalamu alaikum. How are you? I am participating in this year's EPC contest. The topic for this year is about peace and justice in Islam. I like this topic because it is very interesting. I am learning a lot about what it means to be a peaceful person in Islam and how the Prophet Muhammad (SAWS) was a great example for us. I would like to share some things I learned with you. First of all, Islam means submission to Allah, which gives us peace in our hearts and minds. Also, one of Allah's names is Al- Salaam, which means the Giver of peace. Secondly, the Prophet (SAWS) was sent to the world as a mercy to mankind. Allah says this in Surah Anbiya,

"And We have not sent you, [O Muhammad], except as a mercy to the worlds." [Al-Quran, 21:107]

Both of these mean that Islam is a peaceful religion. Being peaceful means that we are friendly and kind towards everyone and that we don't start fights. It also means that we forgive people and that we love everyone for the sake of Allah. The make Allah very happy with us.

Qasim, there are many stories of the Prophet (SAWS) where he is nice and peaceful. One story was a bout a non-Muslim lady who used to throw garbage on the Prophet (SAWS). She used to do it every day but one day she was sick. The prophet (SAWS) actually went to visit her. He was so nice to her that she became Muslim right away. Another story is when a poor man gave the Prophet (SAWS) grapes and when he tasted them, they were sour. However, the Prophet (SAWS) did not make a face while eating them. The

Prophet (SAWS) did not want to hurt the poor man's feelings. Both of these stories show how the Prophet (SAWS) stayed peaceful.

Peace in Islam is very important because Allah does not want us to fight. Since you and I are friends, Qasim, I hope we never fight and always love each other for the sake of Allah.

Your friend

Young Muslim Voices

2nd place: Merium Ahmad
Homeschool, Lanham, MD

December 29, 2020

Bismillah
Dear Jenna,

Assalamu alaikum. How are you? I was thinking about what happened yesterday, when we had the huge fight with Sarah. I think we should give her a card to say sorry. I told my mom what happened, and she got sad. She told me the Prophet (SAWS) said,

"A Muslim is the one who avoids harming Muslims with his tongue and hands." [Sahih Al-Bukhari]

Islam means peace, so Muslims have to be peaceful with others. You know, even though she said bad stuff to us we should not have done the same to her. One day, Prophet Muhammad (SAWS) and Abu Bakar (RA) were sitting under a tree. Then a man came to Abu Bakar and said bad stuff to him, and Abu Bakar stayed quiet. The Prophet (SAWS) smiled. Then Abu Bakar (RA) said something back to defend himself, and the Prophet (SAWS) stopped smiling and walked away. Abu Bakar ran to him and asked him why he left. He (SAWS) said,

"When you were quiet, an angel came to defend you. But when you talked back the angel left." [Musnad Ahmad]

This shows us it is better to not argue back.

I told my mom my idea to give Sarah a card. Tell me what you think. Come over tomorrow and we can make it together inshaAllah.

Wasalamu alaykom
LOVE XXX

3rd Place: Milan Harris Kamal
Al-Rahmah School, Baltimore, MD

January 1, 2020
Dear Brother,
Assalamu alaikum,

The word Islam is derived from the word "Silm" which means "Peace". The Prophet Muhammad (SAWS) said:

"A Muslim is the one who avoids harming Muslims with his tongue and hands." [Sahih Al-Bukhari]

An old woman used to throw trash at the path of Prophet Muhammad (SAWS). One day the women did not show up to throw trash at him. Prophet Muhammad (SAWS) went to her house and noticed that she was sick. The woman thought that Prophet Muhammad (SAWS) had come to her home to take revenge. Prophet Muhammed (SAWS) told her that he had come to see her as Allah has commanded him to visit anyone who is sick. The old woman was deeply impacted by this gesture and converted to Islam.

There are many examples in ahadith about the Prophet Muhammad (SAWS) promoting peace. In one of the Hadith quoted in Sunan Ibn Majah, the Prophet Muhammad (SAWS) said:

"Spread (the greeting of) Salam, offer food (to the needy), and be brothers as Allah, the Mighty and Sublime, has honored you." [Sunan Ibn Majah]

Once a man asked Prophet Muhammad (SAWS) "Which act in Islam is the best?" He replied, "To give food, and to greet everyone, whether you know or you do not." [Sahih Al-Bukhari and Al-Muslim]

I hope these examples help you understand that the Prophet Muhammad (SAWS) had a vision to promote peace amongst human beings in the world. I hope we can all follow the Sunnah of the Prophet in our lives.

Your Brother

Young Muslim Voices

Special Recognition – Essay: Saim Hasan
Washington International Academy, Springfield, VA

Dear Mother,

Assalamu alaikum, how are you? I am fine.

I wanted to tell you what I learned from you about Prophet Muhammad's (SAWS) peaceful personality.

Peace is the opposite of fighting and bullying. Peace means being fair and friendly. It is important to be peaceful because being peaceful helps you be a much better person and helps you to have many friends.

I will tell you a story about Prophet Muhammad (SAWS) that I learned from you.

There was a neighbor who always tried to hurt and bother Prophet Muhammad (SAWS) by throwing garbage on top of him whenever he would pass by. One day Prophet Muhammad (SAWS) went out of his house, but the neighbor did not throw garbage on him and so Prophet Muhammad (SAWS) became worried about his neighbor. He went to find out what happened to his neighbor because he wanted to make sure that she was okay and help if there was any need. When she met Prophet Muhammad (SAWS), she felt bad and was extremely embarrassed because of all the bad things she did to him. She was surprised that he wanted to take care of her. She was so happy, and she decided to become a Muslim and follow Prophet Muhammad (SAWS) and believe in Allah.

From this story, I learned to be patient with everyone but especially with those people who do not like me and try to bother me. Thank you for teaching me this amazing story!

Love,
Your Son

Special Recognition – Speech: Zainab AbdulBasit
Tarbiyah Academy, Elkridge, MD

Dear Dada Abbu and Dado,

I hope you are doing well. I wanted to share a story with you about the mercy of Allah and our Prophet (SAWS). This story begins when the Prophet (SAWS) visited the city of Taif with his servant Zaid to invite them to Islam. He stayed there for three days, and nobody paid attention to his message, and they treated him badly. Then they sent their children and slaves to hit the Prophet (SAWS) and Zaid when they were leaving Taif. He was bleeding when he left the city. He was sad and he prayed to Allah. Angel Gibriel came to him and asked him if he orders the mountains around the city of Taif will crush the whole city. The merciful and peaceful Prophet (SAWS) said no. Instead, he prayed that their children follow Islam one day.

This story shows how peaceful Allah and Prophet are. How Allah did not destroy the people of Taif after what they did and how the Prophet (SAWS) prayed for them. I hope all Muslims follow this example and we all live peacefully.

Allah Hafiz!

ELEMENTARY SCHOOL | LEVEL 2

Topic:

The way of Prophet Muhammad (SAWS) was to be kind, peaceful and just. In what ways do you try and follow Prophet Muhammad's (SAWS) example to maintain peace and justice when interacting with others? What are some of the situations in which you are trying to be a "peaceful Muslim"? Is it difficult to keep up and maintain peace and be just in the environment you live in? How does a peaceful nature help build your identity?

This poster was submitted by Azwa of level 2.

1st Place: Yusuf Mehmood
MCC, Silver Spring, MD

Ring, ring, ring! The bell is ringing, it is time for our school tour. Welcome to Peace University. Today's topic is...you guessed it: Peace! My name is Yusuf Mehmood. I will be your teacher for today. Have you heard of the word Salam? It comes from the Arabic root word letters SEEN LAAM MEEM. Salam means peace. Our religion Islam also comes from this root word as this is the religion of peace.

We will walk through 3 classrooms today in which you will learn about peace in 3 different settings as they relate to Islam. The first classroom you will tour will be peace as a Muslim within your family. The second classroom will teach about peace and justice in the community. The third classroom will teach about peace in the world. Let's begin our tour!

The first classroom teaches about peace within the family. There are many ways to have peace within your home and family. Allah is pleased with us if our parents are pleased with us. We should never talk back to our parents and always talk to them with respect. Your parents may even have a different religion than you, but you still need to respect them and behave peacefully with them. Also, with your siblings learn to share and not fight with them. I have 2 sisters in my home, and I always try my best to share my toys with them. When we play game boards, sometimes an argument is about to start but I tell myself to slowly breathe in and breathe out and say 'Authobillah". This technique helps me to stay peaceful and patient. So, feel free to look around this classroom where they teach peace within the family.

On to our second classroom in Peace University. This classroom teaches about peace in the community. In Islam, we are one Ummah or one nation with different races and ethnicities. In the Quran Allah says:

"O mankind, indeed, We have created you from male and female and made you peoples and tribes that you may know one another. Indeed, the most noble of you in the sight of Allah is the most righteous[1] of you. Indeed, Allah is Knowing and Aware." [Al-Quran; 49:13]

This ayah shows that we need to be united and kind to one another. If we are not peaceful amongst each other how can we be supportive to one another? Outside of the Muslim community, we need to be peaceful to EVERYONE. I try to be kind to my neighbors, once my neighbor's mailbox fell. My dad and I helped him screw it back on. Our Prophet (SAWS) was very peaceful with his neighbors. There was a lady who used to throw trash on his path, one day there was no trash. Instead of being happy, he became worried and went to visit her. She was sick and was so surprised that the same person she tortured had come to visit her. She immediately accepted Islam after she saw the peace of Islam. Another example of being peaceful in the community is being respectful to the elderly. I visit a nursing home in Silver Spring 4 times a year.

I spend time with them, read books to them, bake cookies with them, learn to crochet and sometimes even sing for them. This brings a lot of peace to my heart. When I help people in the community, I know that I am spreading peace and love.

Our third and final classroom teaches about peace in the world. This is at a large-scale level. We can all make a difference in the world by taking care of small things like recycling or planting trees. My grandfather loves to plant flowers and trees. The birds come and sit on the branches and sing peaceful tunes. This helps the environment by making the air clean. When I grow up, I want to help with the law so I can help spread peace. If peaceful laws exist, then there will be less violence and killings. Less kids will become refugees and orphans. If everyone attended Peace University, the world would be a better place.

I hope you enjoyed this thorough tour of Peace University. I hope it will open your hearts to bring peace to your family, to your community and to the world. If you want to find peace within yourself, you must learn to spread peace to others as well. I hope you will apply these concepts of respect, patience and kindness in your lives. And maybe, someday we will all change the world together and make the earth a peaceful place.

2nd Place: Musa Rahmani
Washington International Academy, Alexandria, VA

Islam teaches us that it is very important to be peaceful and just. I think being a peaceful person means to be kind, loving, and compassionate and that justice means treating people equally. I try to be a peaceful and just Muslim by always being honest, having good manners, talking respectfully with others, and by standing up for others. I try to be this way with everyone around me, even if I don't know them and even if they are not Muslim. It is important to speak up for peace and justice for others because we are all human beings created by Allah (SWT).

It is also Sunnah to be peaceful and just. There was once a woman who would throw trash in front of Prophet Muhammad's home. One day, the Prophet (SAWS) noticed that she had stopped and found out that she was sick. He visited her and helped her with some things that she needed but could not do because she was sick. Later, she became a Muslim because of his kind actions. An example of when the Prophet Muhammad (SAWS) showed justice was when he decided how the black stone should be placed into the Kabah. He made a decision that was fair to everyone because he said that one person from every tribe should hold the cloth that the black stone was in and place it in the Kabah together. Throughout his entire life, the Prophet Muhammad (SAWS) had many examples of being peaceful and just because he had a beautiful character, Ma shaa Allah.

It is sometimes hard to act peacefully and with justice because something might annoy you. Everyone gets mad or frustrated sometimes. But as Muslims we should remember that the Prophet Muhammad (SAWS) was always peaceful and just. One time, one of my friends said something that hurt my feelings. But I didn't say anything mean back to him and I made an excuse for him because he might have just been frustrated. When it was class time later on, and we had five minutes to answer some questions that he hadn't finished yet, I helped him. It was the fair thing to do since I had already finished my questions, even though it was hard to because he had hurt my feelings.

My teacher demonstrates peace and justice every day when she is always patient with us. She also helps us solve our problems fairly by telling us not to argue and instead talk our problems out together. My parents always tell me stories of how the Prophet Muhammad (SAWS) and other Prophets showed peace and justice when they were all spreading the message of Islam. Having a peaceful and just character is important for us all because we will become closer to Allah (SWT) who will give us more blessings. We will also be closer to the Prophet Muhammad (SAWS) because we will be following his Sunnah which means we will be closer to achieving Jannah, Inshallah!

3rd Place: Hamza-Syed Ali
Home School, Gaithersburg, MD

The Prophet Muhammad (SAWS) was an ideal example of representing kindness, peaceful and just throughout his lifetime. Whether it was interacting with his family members or anybody that the Prophet (SAWS) would come across. Keeping this in mind I would like to develop these characteristics within, to better myself. Not only for my parents but also for everybody around me whether it is family or friends. Being a peaceful Muslim in difficult situations would help to maintain these characteristics that I am looking forward to developing in my life.

Throughout my life I have experienced many situations where I have tried to be kind towards other, while maintaining just and peacefulness. One example, when I am interacting with others, I try to follow the footsteps of the Prophet Muhammad (SAWS) by is if somebody tries to call me by bad names, in response I just listen to them peacefully without saying anything bad back to them. Even after that if they try to be mean to me, I try to be nice to them and help in any way possible. One of my favorite examples of the Prophet (SAWS) maintaining peace and justice was when the Prophet (SAWS) would walk on the same path every single day and an old lady would throw garbage on top of the Prophet's (SAWS) head, as well as the pathway that he would walk on. This would cause the Prophet (SAWS) many difficulties, but he would maintain peace by not reacting or saying anything bad back to the old lady. So, one day when he walked the same pathway the old lady didn't throw any garbage so knowing the nature of the Prophet (SAWS) he went up to the old lady's house looking for her. When the Prophet (SAWS) came to the old lady's house he found out that she is extremely sick so that's why she didn't throw the garbage that day and the Prophet (SAWS) asked her how she was without making her feel bad about anything. In the end the old lady became a Muslim by seeing how a Muslim treats others.

This also shows how a peaceful Muslim should behave in difficult situations by always maintaining his/her peace when interacting with people he/she may not get along with. This story has inspired me in many ways that I can maintain a peaceful and kind nature towards others. Another example, I try to be just with people that I interact with such as my little cousins when they take my cookies without asking me or even any supplies, I still try to be kind to them and let them share my stuff happily.

These are some of the examples that show how I have maintained my kindness, peacefulness and justice while interacting with others around me on a daily basis. Knowing the life of the Prophet (SAWS) helps me maintain these qualities within myself to improve my life. Overall, I have developed a positive overlook on life by keeping these characteristics and following them throughout my life.

Special Recognition – Essay: Sumayyah Ahmad
Home School, Herndon, VA

This essay is about peace. Allah sent us the book of Guidance, the Quran. The Quran teaches us to be patient, peaceful, merciful and tons more. If there are bad people, deal with them or fight them.

One day, the Prophet (SAWS) was invited by a non-Muslim, Jewish lady to her house. The lady was not sure the Prophet (SAWS) was a prophet, so she put poison inside the baby lamb. When the Prophet (SAWS) was about to start eating the lamb, the lamb started talking to the Prophet (SAWS). It said, "Do not eat me, the lady put poison inside of me." A Sahabi next to the Prophet (SAWS) died. When she came, the Prophet (SAWS) asked her if it was true that she put poison, and she said yes. The Prophet (SAWS) forgave her, and she became Muslim.

Another time, the Prophet (SAWS) went to Taif. He hoped that the people will become Muslim. Instead, the leaders told the children to chase the Prophet (SAWS) and to throw rocks at the Prophet (SAWS). The Prophet (SAWS) was very hurt even though one of the Prophet's (SAWS) sahabas was guarding the Prophet (SAWS). The Prophet (SAWS) was so hurt that his feet were stuck to his shoes because there was blood in between his feet and shoes. After a lot of walking, the Prophet (SAWS) was tired, so he found a tree and sat under it. After a little amount of time, Jibreel (AS) came to the Prophet (SAWS) and asked him, "Should I crush both of the mountains so everyone in Taif will get destroyed?" The Prophet (SAWS) said, "No, I hope that one day these children will become Muslim." If it were you, for example, I do not think that you would do that? I won't do that either because we aren't as good as the Prophet (SAWS). The whole of Taif became Muslim. The moral of the story is if people are bad to you, you should not be bad to them because they might become Muslim or they might become better.

There were two brothers named Habil and Qabil. One day, Habil and Qabil sacrificed to Allah, but only Habil's got accepted. Qabil was angry. He told Habil that he was going to kill him. Habil told his brother "Allah only accepts from the righteous who fear him." And then Habil said to his brother "If you try to kill me, I will not kill you, I only fear Allah." After some time Qabil was very angry. He killed Habil. He was very regretful for what he did to Habil.

These stories teach us stuff like to forgive in the first story, and to be patient in the second story, and to be merciful. Peaceful means that you should always be nice to people. You should be peaceful because the Prophet (SAWS) was a peaceful person and if you do bad things, you might become a bad person and go to hellfire.

Special Recognition – Speech: Mustafaa Ahmed
M&M Learning Center, College Park, MD

I love Islam because it is a religion of peace. If anyone wants to have peace in their lives, they should become a Muslim. Becoming a Muslim does not mean you are turning into an alien. It means that you believe in Allah and agree to follow everything He teaches us so that we can get to Jannah. The Prophet Muhammad (SAWS) also taught us how to act with people. He was sent as a *"mercy to mankind"*, as Allah says in Surah Al-Anbiyah, Ayah 107. In the news, many people make it seem like Islam is a religion that promotes war and fighting but that is not true. I know this because Allah teaches us to be good and kind to one another. We are only supposed to fight someone if they are fighting us. The Prophet Muhammad (SAWS) also taught us to always use kind words and patience when dealing with other people.

I always wonder why people have to be mean to one another. It is not easy to stay nice all of the time, especially when someone is saying bad things to you or constantly annoying you, but this is why we have the Quran and the teachings of the Prophet (SAWS). Allah (SWT) teaches us that patience is always a characteristic that Allah loves. The Prophet Muhammad (SAWS) taught us that we should be kind to each other no matter what. One of the stories that I really like about the Prophet (SAWS) is about the woman who used to throw trash on his head every day while he walked past her house. She would throw trash on him for days. One day, she was not there to throw trash on him, and the Prophet (SAWS) went to check up on her. She turned out to be sick and the Prophet (SAWS) helped her out. She was amazed by his kindness and became Muslim. That was amazing, Ma shaa Allah Allah. Another story is about an old woman who was in the desert and walking while carrying luggage on her head. The Prophet (SAWS) took the luggage and started carrying it for her. He asked her where she was going, and she told him that she heard there was a magician in town and that she did not want to be in town anymore. She kept complaining about this "magician", not knowing that she was talking about the Prophet (SAWS).

The Prophet (SAWS) listened so patiently without saying a word. Once they reached her destination, she asked the Prophet his name. The Prophet (SAWS) said "I am Muhammad, the one you were complaining about". The woman could not believe that such a nice person could be a magician and could cause any trouble, so she accepted Islam. These stories show how patient the Prophet (SAWS) was even when people were not being nice to him. And because of this, two women accepted Islam. This is the best thing that could have happened, Alhamdulillah!

My parents are always telling me and my brothers and sisters that we have to start being peaceful with each other at home first because that is where we can practice being patient and kind. I am number 6 of 9 brothers and sisters so there are usually a lot of situations going on. To me, being peaceful and just means to share my things with my younger siblings, to have good manners with my older siblings and to not yell at anyone even if they are yelling at me. At school, there was a time when I was accidentally sitting in another kid's seat. He is bigger than me and he just picked me up off the chair and threw me to the floor. I got hurt and felt embarrassed, but I told him nicely that he should not bully people like that. I wanted to yell at him but for some reason, I found myself just being calm. Later, the teacher punished him because of what he did, and he did not bother me again. At my age, my parents say that using kind words and just treating everyone with respect is all that matters. This is how we learn to be good Muslims and as we get older, we develop good habits when dealing with other people. Being peaceful brings a lot of barakah from Allah and prevents us from worrying about things too much. If we always try to do the right thing, Allah will guide us in sha Allah.

This is what being peaceful and just means to me. I think that if everyone started thinking about their actions, we would not have a lot of fighting in the world.

MIDDLE SCHOOL | LEVEL 3

Topic:

What does it mean to stay peaceful and be just in our everyday undertakings? Why should one maintain peace and be just being a Muslim? What do prophetic teachings and Allah's (SWT) commandments demand from you and why should you maintain it? What are the common traps that can lead one to the path of violence and injustice? What are the consequences for not striving to attain peace and justice in our dealings with others? How can you confront violence, hatred, and injustice with your own words and actions as a Muslim?

Young Muslim Voices

1st Place: Mariyah Mehmood
MCC, Silver Spring, MD

Welcome to Salam's Pizza shop! Have you ever thought of the peace symbol as a pizza? Let me teach you about today's special, the Peace Pizza. First of all, the Arabic word for peace is Salam. Salam comes from the Arabic root letters of Seen, Laam, Meem. Islam also comes from these root words because it is the religion of peace. Ok this next concept involves some math skills. Imagine the pizza is split in thirds. Each third is as follows: family peace slice, community peace slice and world peace slice. The community peace slice is divided once again in half into: Muslim community and non- Muslim community peace slices. Each part of this pizza comes together to make a whole pie. If one slice is missing, then it is no longer the Peace Pizza! As a Muslim, it is my duty to spread peace to my family, community and the world.

SLICE 1: FAMILY PEACE SLICE   SLICE 4: WORLD PEACE SLICE

SLICES 2 and 3 COMMUNITY PEACE SLICES:
MUSLIM AND NONMUSLIM COMMUNITIES

Let's taste the yummy slice #1: Family Peace Slice. When preparing this slice, you need to have quite a few important toppings. You need peace towards siblings. Some examples from my life include not fighting with them, letting them choose the TV channel, helping my sister choose her clothes and letting my sister use my body sprays. I know that being peaceful and patient with my brother and sister will allow my parents to relax as well. Rasul Allah (SAWS) was very kind and peaceful to his family. Aisha (RA) reported: The Messenger of Allah (SAWS) said,

"The best of you is he who is best to his family, and I am the best among you to my family." [Sunan At-Tirmidhi]

With my parents, I show the utmost respect. I do not raise my voice and listen to everything they say. I make my mother tea when she is tired and help my father make French toast on Saturday mornings. I help my family to create a peaceful environment in our home.

Slices 2 and 3 have very special toppings and must be made with love and care. These are the slices for peace in the community. In the Muslim community we can spread peace by treating all Muslims with respect. It does not matter what race or skin color you have; we are all children of Adam. Racism and bullying should not be tolerated in the Muslim community. This builds barriers amongst us, and we will never be united. I also try my best to spread salam.

2nd Place: Tasneem Syeda Ali
Home School, Gaithersburg, MD

Islam is an eternal religion for all people. Islam is a complete way of life that provides the code of conduct for everything we do and say. The two sources that guide us to the straight path are the Qur'an and the Sunnah. The Qur'an contains the Kalimatullah. The importance of the Sunnah is explained by this Qur'an ayah:

"He who obeys the Messenger has obeyed Allah..." [Al-Quran; 4:80]

By following Islam, we can help promote peace and justice in the world.

How do we apply Islamic ideals of peace and justice as practiced by RasulAllah (SAWS) in our time? We begin our interactions with people in a peaceful way by exchanging the appropriate greeting. Then, we should work on the context of our conversation. When dealing with others we must not argue, even if we are correct. Abu Umamah narrated that RasulAllah (SAWS) said:

"I guarantee a house in the surroundings of Paradise for a man who avoids quarreling even if he were in the right..." [Sunan Abi Dawud]

What does this mean? We should be thoughtful about the words we utter when speaking. We can avoid words with negative connotations, harsh tones, and those that incite conflict.

Now we have a basic idea of how we should engage in conversations, let us focus on conduct with others. What does Islam say about how we should conduct ourselves within our families? As a building block of society, we can learn about how to deal with others in our interactions within our families. From the sunnah, we learn not to let minor disagreements turn into big arguments that can ruin family ties where people stop speaking with one another. Jubair-bin-Mut'im narrates, he heard RasulAllah (SAWS) saying,

'The person who severs the bond of kinship will not enter Paradise." [Sahih Al-Bukhari]

This teaches us that while we might disagree with someone, we must not let that ruin our relationship and risk sacrificing Jannah. Another important lesson we learn from the Prophet (SAWS) is helping our families. Al-Aswad-bin-Yazid narrated, "I asked 'Aisha' what RasulAllah (SAWS) used to do at home?' She said,

"He used to work for his family, and when he heard the Adhan, he would go out." [Sahih Al-Bukhari]

Even though RasulAllah (SAWS) had an important mission, he still found time to help with household chores. In our busy world today, this serves as an important lesson. No matter how busy we are, our families deserve our time and attention.

Our neighborhoods provide an excellent place to demonstrate our faith in action. Abu Hurayrah narrates that RasulAllah (SAWS) said:

"Jibril kept enjoining good treatment of neighbors until I thought he would make neighbors heirs." [Sunan Ibn- Majah]

What we learn from this is we need to be kind to our neighbors since they are almost as close to us as family. This is true even if they are not Muslim. We must share food with our neighbors, help them, and look after their property when they are away. By practicing Islam at this level in our neighborhoods we help spread the beauty of Islam.

3rd Place: Raid Bhuyan
Tarbiyah Academy, Elkridge, MD

What does "Peace" mean? "Peace" means freedom from disturbance which is the state of tranquility of the environment and everything in it. Quran and Sunnah has the guidelines and teachings of how we can be peaceful. How I can try to stay peaceful and just to those around me by applying those teachings.

What are some ways we as Muslims are peaceful? I can read verses that talk about peace in the Quran like,

"The believers are but brothers, so make settlement between your brothers. And fear Allah that you may receive mercy." [Al-Quran; 49:10]

The Prophet (SAWS) showed examples of being peaceful by the way he acted. In the hadith he said, "Shall I not inform you of something more excellent in degree than fasting, prayer and almsgiving (sadaqah)? The people replied: Yes, Prophet of Allah! He said:

"It is putting things right between people, spoiling them is the shaver (destructive)." [Sunan Abi Dawud]

I can be peaceful by using the Prophet's (SAWS) example and the Quran to guide me.

Why is peace important? It is important because if we have no peace then there will be wars, arguments, and fighting. And external problems cause internal problems. And if you have no peace internally, then you will always be angry and unhappy. And your behavior will change those around you, and it will change those around them.

Why is having no peace a bad thing? If there is no peace anywhere, then everyone will be unhappy. That will cause arguments, cheating, and war between countries. And if wars start people will start to die. But if I keep myself at peace by doing things that might help me stay at peace, I won't be angry and frustrated. So, it is important to follow the sunnah of the prophet. Listening to the Quran might help too. Doing calming things like drawing or being alone. If I can be peaceful those around me will be too.

What can I do about being peaceful? I can read the Quran, Follow the prophet's teachings. So, I can be peaceful to those around me. So, I can help prevent hatred, wars and arguments.

Special Recognition – Essay: Ammaar Syed
ADAMS Center, Herndon, VA

Peace and justice are cornerstones for a successful life and a rewarding Hereafter. A lot of people say they want peace, and they claim to be just. But do they really know what it takes to stay peaceful and to be just?

Let's say you're walking down the street minding your own business, and somebody pushes you hard and says, "go back to your country!". You look at the person in shock and think, "why is he or she saying that to me? Is that because of how I look? Should I retaliate in kind for what that person did to me?

Instead, I decide to stay calm, I smile, and I say, "Salaam" while thinking about the Ayah in Surah Furqaan:

"And the servants of the Most Merciful are those who walk upon the earth easily (gently, with dignity but without arrogance) and when the ignorant address them [harshly], they say [words of] peace (or safety)." *[Al- Quran; 25:63]*

With this calm reaction from me, the person is bound to be curious about why I responded that way and could potentially wonder what the word "Salaam" means? Here you have a potential opportunity to explain yourself and your faith. This way I will not only stay peaceful but also not commit any injustice against that person.

Let's take another example. I am generally very possessive about my belongings… my toys, my room etc. If one of my siblings were to enter my room without my permission, I tend to get irritated. But if I ask myself, how can I maintain my peace without treating my sibling unjustly by yelling at and arguing with them, I could instead greet them with *Salaam* (peace) and invite them to share a candy with me. That way, I would maintain my peace as well as be fair and just to my siblings!

Why don't we have peace in the world right now? There is no peace in the world right now because everyone is hungry for power. People will go to any extent or measure to get more power. If people were to follow a principled life, then there will be peace and justice all around.

Have you ever seen someone littering? Do you think they were being just to the environment? No, they weren't. Littering is just one way of doing injustice to our environment. One of the ways I try to be just to my surroundings is by recycling waste at home as well as at the Masjid. This makes me feel at peace with myself.

Another way of doing injustice to those around us is by being an unfair/partial judge. Sometimes judges accept bribes and do injustice to the innocent.

"O you who have believed, be persistently standing firm in justice, witnesses for Allah, even if it be against yourselves or parents and relatives. Whether one is rich or poor, Allah is more worthy of both.[1] So follow not [personal] inclination, lest you not be just. And if you distort [your testimony] or refuse [to give it], then indeed Allah is ever, of what you do, Aware." [Al-Quran; 4:135]

The root word of Islam is "silm" meaning "making peace". According to Islam, peace is the rule and war is only an exception. As a Muslim I strive to balance peace and justice in my life.

Young Muslim Voices

Special Recognition – Speech: Hafsah Khan
Clarksville Elementary School, Clarksville, MD

How can you and I be peaceful throughout our lives? Well, for me, I try to follow the Quran and hadith. Let me start with a story.

It was a bright sunny day at my school. As I go down the slide in our playground, I see a kid in front of me. I look at him and I obviously know he is from a higher grade. He says mean things to me, and I am really sad that he is being mean. I tell him "Please go away. It is not nice to say that." After getting annoyed, he goes to another classmate of mine and tells her the same thing. Confused, I know it's not my business, but it is because he has to stop bullying. He tells me "I'll listen to you this time, but not the next." Later, next year he got suspended. I also told him to "stay calm and be peaceful." Well, in my own words.

How does Allah portray peace and justice in the Quran? Allah (SWT) says in places all over the Quran like,

"Indeed, Allah orders justice and good conduct and giving [help] to relatives and forbids immorality and bad conduct and oppression. He admonishes you that perhaps you will be reminded." [Al-Quran; 16:90]

Allah portrays peace in the Quran such as,

"The believers are but brothers, so make settlement between your brothers. And fear Allah that you may receive mercy." [Al-Quran; 49:10]

It is mentioned more times even in the smallest surahs. Is it mentioned in Hadith too??

Yes, it is mentioned in the Hadith. The prophet (SAWS) said,

"Shall I not inform you of something more excellent in degree than fasting, prayer and almsgiving (sadaqah)? The people replied: Yes, Prophet of Allah! He said: It is putting things right between people, spoiling them is the shaver (destructive)." [Sunan Abi Dawud]

For Justice, it is mentioned by the Prophet (SAWS),

"A day of just leadership is better than sixty years of worship..." [Al-Sunan Al-Kubra]

My daily life also revolves around world peace. As humans, we have to do a lot to bring peace to our planet. There is so much disturbance to people in the world. In Yemen, Syria, India, and Palestine. I really feel that all the organizations out there are doing good, but we need to push ourselves to make peace in those countries and help the fundraisers. There will be peace in the world and people can enjoy everything the way we enjoy today over here. What else can we do to bring or at least try to bring peace?

We can also support protests or even spread a message. Send messages to friends etc. In Palestine today, kids, adults and even the elderly are risking their lives to live. Some even die of pain, suffering, and unjustness. Everywhere there are people who make the world the worst place for us and the best place for them. I love saying this quote: "Aren't we all humans? Then why can't we live with peace?

Quotes about peace really brighten me up. That's because I try to mention them and most importantly, I try to follow them and use them with people around me. Another quote I like to use is:

"Worrying does not take away tomorrow's trouble but it also takes away today's peace."

There are some quotes that I think everyone should use when trouble or cruel things happen. One of them was quoted by Gandhi and that is:

"There is no path to peace, peace is the path."

I love that quote very much. Another one of my favorites is:

"One day, I want to turn on the news and hear, there is peace on earth!"

Quotes about things really help us. Probably one night I search for a quote and the next day I pass it to my friends, and they pass it on etc. It might go viral and inshaAllah there will be peace in this world. I always hear "Peace begins with a smile." My family and friends tell us: "Smile! It's sunnah!" Whenever I am not in the red zone, I keep a smile on my face and remember, Oh hey! At least I am spreading peace to people around me and following the sunnah.

I'm pretty sure we all learned a thing or two today. InshaAllah I hope we all keep a smile on our face at all times (Ameen)! We should all remember and always remember that only Allah (SWT) can bring peace in this world.

MIDDLE SCHOOL | LEVEL 4

Topic:

What does it mean to stay peaceful and be just in our everyday undertakings? Why should one maintain peace and be just being a Muslim? What do prophetic teachings and Allah's (SWT) commandments demand from you and why should you maintain it? What are the common traps that can lead one to the path of violence and injustice? What are the consequences for not striving to attain peace and justice in our dealings with others? How can you confront violence, hatred, and injustice with your own words and actions as a Muslim?

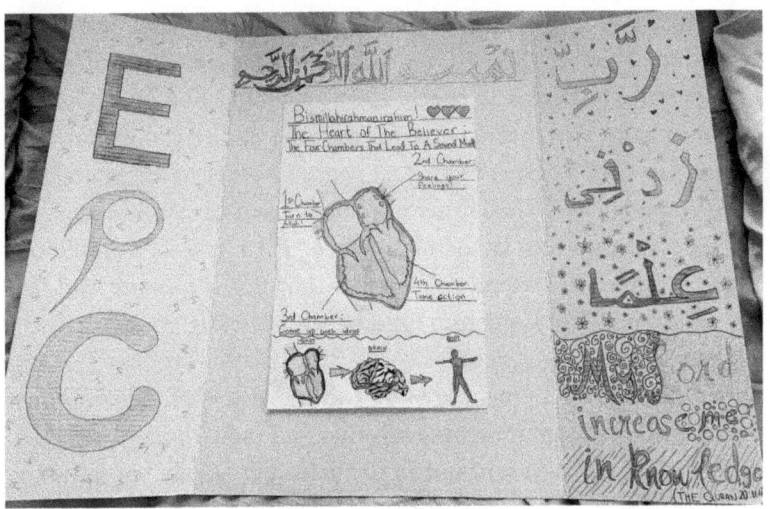

This poster was submitted by Mariya Mehmood of level 4.

1st Place: AbdurRahman Ahmad
Home School, Herndon, VA

"No justice, no peace. Know justice, know peace."

The streets of Washington DC are packed every weekend with protesters protesting the genocides in Kashmir, China, Palestine, Yemen, and many more places around the globe. In my essay, I am going to talk about the levels of peace and justice, how I can maintain peace and justice in every place I go, and how to maintain global peace. Peace is a very broad topic. The dictionary definition for peace is "freedom from disturbance; tranquility". Allah (SWT) says in the Quran:

"Truly, the religion with Allah is Islam." [Al-Quran; 3:19]

Islam has many meanings such as submission and peace. We need Islam to bring peace. If we submit to the will of Allah and the teachings of the Prophet (SAWS), we will achieve peace. The problem in today's world is there is no peace. You hear about a bombing here and a shooting there, but we do nothing to stop it. Peace is not a physical thing. You need a state of spiritual peace in order to act peacefully. The Prophet (SAWS) had inner peace, so he was always peaceful. He is the best example for us to follow. Once, when he went to Taif looking for people who would follow him, they threw him out and had the children of Taif stone him until he was bleeding and hurt. Then, Allah sent the Angel Gibreel (AS) who told the Prophet (SAWS) that if he wanted the people of Taif to be destroyed, he could just make the two mountains come together and they would be crushed. The Prophet (SAWS) said not to because, inshaAllah, someday the children would become Muslim. If that was any other person, he/she would totally destroy the town of Taif. There are many levels of peace, and the Prophet (SAWS) is a good example in all of them, such as peace at home, peace in the neighborhood, peace between different countries, and global peace.

I can maintain a level of peace in my house by being peaceful. It takes two to start a fight, so if you get into a fight with one of your siblings, you can't completely blame them. There is a story in the Quran that talks about the two sons of Adam. They both made a sacrifice, and it was accepted from one of them and it wasn't accepted from the second one. He got angry and said, "I am going to kill you." The younger brother was peaceful and said, "if you raise your hand to kill me, I will not retaliate". The older brother killed his younger brother, who did not defend himself. If one of your siblings is mean to you, you should act like the younger brother did. He became among the righteous because he was peaceful. You can maintain peace in your community by seeing why there isn't peace and working to help the community gain that. Let's give ADAMS Center as an example. Let's say their prayer times are wrong, then you could help them by offering to fix it before someone gets mad at ADAMS Center for having the wrong prayer times, which would disrupt the peace in ADAMS Center.

Let's say there is a war between America and North Korea. That would disrupt a lot of peace. A few ways you can work towards stopping the war would be to write a letter to the president telling him to stop, protest, and ask your parents to vote in the next election for someone who will stop the war. And if there is a world war then the most you can do is to make dua. The Prophet (SAWS) said,

"Whosoever of you sees an evil, let him change it with his hand; and if he is not able to do so, then [let him change it] with his tongue; and if he is not able to do so, then with his heart — and that is the weakest of faith." [Sahih Al-Muslim]

The Prophet (SAWS) is a good example for us in maintaining peace everywhere. If we are able to maintain global peace, that would be one of the world's greatest triumphs. No one would be fighting, and the big countries could spend their money on something other than weapons. To maintain global peace, you need to start with having peace in your own heart, then your home, and then your country.

2nd Place: Nahshmia Jaharan
ADAMS Center, Sterling, VA

When I was memorizing the Qur'an, our teacher would assign a short essay every week. It was not just any type of essay, but it was about what the Khateeb said during Jumu'ah. If we didn't go to Jumu'ah that week, we would have to write about how we can improve our behavior. One day, I sat down to read all the Jumu'ah Khutbah essays. After reading the whole notebook, I realized that even though all the khutbahs had different topics, they all had several things in common, and one of them was bringing peace. But what is peace? Peace is the feeling of no disturbance, like calmness and tranquility. Our religion, Islam, and our name, Muslims, come from the word al-silm, meaning peace. If Islam and our name mean peace, shouldn't we be trying to spread peace? In fact, the Prophet (SAWS) said,

"By Him in Whose Hand my soul is! You will not enter Jannah until you believe, and you shall not believe until you love one another. May I inform you of something, if you do, you love each other. Promote greeting amongst you (by saying As-salamu 'alaikum to one another)." [Sahih Muslim]

In this essay, I'll talk about how the earth will be without peace and why we need it, one of the things that people have difficulty dealing with and the solution for it, and finally how I can spread peace.

Without peace, it'll be very hard and maybe even impossible for a single individual to live. Anxiety, stress, anger, and depression take up all the space inside of an individual who lacks peace. The person will then spread it to his friends, and they will also feel disturbed and will unconsciously spread it around, one person to another. The chain will then go on all the way until the earth is covered with disruption and wars, which can make mankind go completely heedless.

This is why we need peace. It is to preserve happiness and health. It is also to help us accomplish what we need to accomplish, and that cannot be done without peace. Peace is actually a gift from Allah, and Allah put us on the earth as Khalifahs. It is true, most of us humans have gone heedless, but many true Muslims are still among us and there are still inshaAllah more of us coming. It is our job to preserve peace. But sometimes it does get hard.

What should our response be when someone says something bad about us? Allah (SWT) says in the Quran in Surah Qasas:

"And when they hear ill speech, they turn away from it and say, "For us are our deeds, and for you are your deeds. Peace will be upon you (you are secure from being treated in a like manner by us); we seek not the ignorant." [Al-Quran; 28:55]

What this means is when someone says something offensive about you, just relax! Say peace! Say we do not desire the company of yours! That is how simple Allah (SWT) made it for us! Yet we go around taking revenge. But this is only if someone offends you. If someone really insults your parents, relatives, or even the Prophet (SAWS), it is okay to say something back, not something so infuriating but something good enough to defend the offended.

A good example of achieving peace is prayer. Allah (SWT) ordered us to pray so we can do dhikr, which gives us peace. A common example of spreading peace at home is when you know your mom will tell you to be quiet, be quiet before she even tells you. At school, act in a way that makes the teacher feel peaceful when she sees you since you do not cause any disturbance. In a community, you can help out by volunteering in a way that gets everything done. In any general place, if any rules are being violated, you can inform the others or be a role model and apply all of the rules.

Bringing peace is a crucial activity that will benefit me and maybe even others in this world and the next. I cannot convince everyone to do right and make peace, but I can try to convince them but at the same time I'll try hard to do good and make peace.

If we keep the main goal, eternal peace and Jannah, it could be easier for others and me to achieve peace.

3rd Place: Heela Keri
Al-Huda School, College Park, MD

In our world today, being peaceful and just is a conflict that has a strong tie between the two. Peace and justice are like a bird with two wings, which cannot fly without the other. Silah reported: 'Ammar Ibn Yasir (RA) said,

> "Whoever has these following three qualities has completed the faith: a sense of fairness in yourself, spending charity despite difficult circumstances, and offering peace to the world". [Musannaf Ibn Abi-Shaybah]

Without a balance, peace and justice would not be obtained. I maintain peace and justice through following these three habits. First, I try to speak good and keep quiet. The Prophet Muhammad (SAWS) said:

> "...whoever believes in Allah and the Last Day, should speak what is good or keep silent." [Sahih Al-Bukhari]

If you have nothing good to say and keep quiet, then you can avoid arguments and fighting. Every good word is counted as a good deed for a Muslim. The tongue is a gift from Allah and should not be used for bad language.

Secondly, I try to be open-minded and fair-minded in a conflict. Making wudu keeps me refreshed and calm to think about the situation. You're not the only one who has beliefs. To be open-minded, you have to know that there are others' beliefs from those around you. To be fair-minded, I always have to remember there are three sides to a story: what I believe, what others believe, and the truth. Allah says in Surah Nisa,

"Indeed, Allah commands you to render trusts to whom they are due and when you judge between people to judge with justice. Excellent is that which Allah instructs you. Indeed, Allah is ever Hearing and Seeing." [Al- Quran; 4:58]

Lastly, always look at the bigger picture. When looking at the main problem you know what to fix first. Running after perfection in this case will not solve anything. Slow down and try thinking things through. Ask for Allah's help by making du'a. Allah is always there to help. Anas Ibn Malik (RA) reported: The Messenger of Allah (SAWS) said,

"Let one of you ask his Lord concerning his needs, all of them, until he asks him even for a shoestring when his breaks." [Sunan At-Tirmidhi]

To wrap it all up, these are ways I maintain peace and justice with those around me. Using the tongue, the right way. Being cautious of those around me. Focusing on the main problem. This will make a big impact on society and let the bird fly. May Allah help us all through conflict and guide us on the right path. Ameen!

Special Recognition – Essay: Ruwad Islam
Al-Huda School, College Park, MD

Being just and maintaining peace is necessary in our daily lives as Muslims. This also gives Muslims a better reputation because, sadly, people think us Muslims are "terrorists". Also, Muslims are oppressed in many parts of the world, which is very sad, because Muslims do not deserve that treatment. However, this is the will of Allah (SWT), and by His will, their suffering will end.

I can be just by telling the truth in all my dealings. If I am honest, Allah will be happy with me. Another benefit to being honest is going to Jannah, as said in this hadith: Abdullah Ibn Mas'ud (RA) reported: The Messenger of Allah (SAWS) said,

"Truthfulness leads to righteousness, and righteousness leads to Paradise. And a man keeps on telling the truth until he becomes a truthful person. Falsehood leads to Al-Fajur (i.e., wickedness, evil-doing), and Al-Fajur (wickedness) leads to the (Hell) Fire, and a man may keep on telling lies till he is written before Allah, a liar." [Sahih Al-Bukhari]

We can conclude from this hadith that the punishment of a liar is severe, so we as Muslims shouldn't lie. I can maintain peace throughout my day by avoiding things like arguments and letting other things upset me. That is one way I stay just throughout my day. Also, maintaining peace and being just means to be kind and fair to anybody- family or strangers, Muslim or non-Muslim- and keeping stability throughout my day. This also brings many rewards, like the pleasure of Allah (SWT). And as said in this hadith, Allah's Messenger (SAWS) said,

"If Allah loves a person, He calls Gabriel, saying, 'Allah loves so and so, O Gabriel love him' So Gabriel would love him and then would make an announcement in the Heavens: 'Allah has loved so and-so

therefore you should love him also.' So, all the dwellers of the Heavens would love him, and then he is granted the pleasure of the people on the Earth." [Sahih al-Bukhari]

What being just and maintaining peace means is to treat everyone equally and keep calm during the day. Muslims should follow these. The life of the Prophet (SAWS) has been said by his wife, Aisha (RA) to be like "a walking Qur'an", embodying the laws of Almighty Allah (SWT). Allah (SWT) and the Prophet (SAWS) both tell us to be peaceful and just. Also, some traps that can lead to unjust and violence are bad influences.

To wrap it all up, maintaining peace is an important part in our daily lives. There are many ahadith and ayahs about this topic. There are many other ways to maintain peace and be just. I only covered a few. This is how I stay just and maintain peace in my daily life.

Young Muslim Voices

Special Recognition – Speech: Huda Javaid
Al-Huda School, College Park, MD

Research shows that a person has the ability to speak around 7,000 to 20,000 words per day. These words leave an impact on the world around you each day. Peacefulness in your environment can be shattered by many things; the simplest of those things is your tongue. The Prophet (SAWS) said,

"...either speak good or remain silent" [Sahih Muslim]

This is a daily reminder to all Muslims that if you do not have anything good to say, it is best to stay quiet. Justice is also a main component in our everyday lives. The Prophet exercised justice when dealing with his companions and the people around him. It is our duty to mimic the Prophet's characteristics in our everyday life in order to live a fulfilling life. Peace and justice are some of the most important aspects of Islam and human nature. Your words, expressions, and our actions can dictate how you are in your society.

The Prophet is someone who always used justice and peace when he dealt with people, he never discriminated against anyone because of race, ethnicity, gender, or class. There are many instances that are recorded by the Sahabah that showcased the Prophet's kindness and compassion towards others. For example, when a Jewish woman in Mecca who would throw garbage on the doorstep of the Prophet's house fell sick, the Prophet visited the lady out of pure concern and kindness within his heart. This justice and compassion led the Jewish woman to embrace Islam as well. We should all aspire to reach this level of grace when dealing with adversity in the name of religion. There was also one quote inscribed on the Prophet's (SAW) sword:

"Forgive those who have wronged you, reconcile with those who have cut you off, show excellence to those who have shown you evil, and speak the truth even if it's against yourself." [Silsilat al-Ahadeeth al-Saheehah]

This signified the true meaning of peace and justice. I've learned that maintaining peace and justice is hard, especially on bad days. In History class I was assigned to be the group leader for a project. Being a group leader meant that I had to maintain peace and be fair to my teammates. But that was hard when no one wanted to pay attention or put in any effort. After a couple of questions, complaints, and a lot of hard work, I became frustrated. Maintaining peace was getting hard and at times like this I thought I was going to explode but I kept my cool and maintained the peace in my group. Dealing with my group in terms of peace and justice all worked out when our project was returned to us, and we all got A's. Maintaining peace and justice to those around you is harder than it looks. So, I have three things that help me in my daily life. First, I take a deep breath in and exhale. It's an important and vital step that many people forget to do in the heat of the moment when dealing with a not-so- peaceful situation. Second, organize your thoughts, think about what you are doing right now and "put into boxes" what you're doing later. Lastly and most importantly, do what's best for what you and other people **need**, not what you and other people **want**. Following other people's desires is what disrupts peace in almost all situations. It's better to stick with what you need, rather than what you want. I hope these helped you as much as they helped me maintain peace and justice to those around you.

Maintaining peace and justice is a vital step to perfecting our Ummah, whether it's at work, at home, or even in your mind. Ibn Al-Qayyim said,

"Whichever path leads to justice is part of Islam and can never oppose it."

This means that justice and peace are major components of the Muslim faith. I try to maintain peace and justice in my everyday life, thus helping me become a better Muslim. But it is good to always remember that the words we say, the expressions we use, and the actions we do will always justify the right from wrong in our society.

HIGH SCHOOL | LEVEL 5

Topic:

What does it mean to stay peaceful and be just in our everyday undertakings? Why should one maintain peace and be just being a Muslim? What do prophetic teachings and Allah's (SWT) commandments demand from you and why should you maintain it? What are the common traps that can lead one to the path of violence and injustice? What are the consequences for not striving to attain peace and justice in our dealings with others? How can you confront violence, hatred, and injustice with your own words and actions as a Muslim?

1st Place: Ahnaf Hossain
ADAMS Center, Sterling, VA

"Indeed, Allah orders justice and good conduct and giving [help] to relatives and forbids immorality and bad conduct and oppression. He admonishes you that perhaps you will be reminded." [Al-Quran; 16:90]

Peace and Justice are quite relative terms. They are defined by many levels and shaped by the views of people around them. The first term, peace, can be internal, where you are not being disturbed by something. It can also be external, as in between humans, communities, and countries.

But peace is not complete without justice. Imagine that a country fights another country, and the oppressor wins. He could throw the country into dictatorship and establish communism, but it is not just, as the slacking technician makes the same as the hardworking one. The just one would speak out against it, would be killed, but he has thrown the flames of revolution to the stacked log pile of oppression. From this, the chant "No Justice, No Peace" would rise, which means that peace, no matter it being with or without war, will never work without justice.

The Prophet (SAWS) has shown us, the Ummah, how to always stay peaceful and just, even if anger or sympathy would have been the easy way out. Some situations in which he was peaceful are based on a hadith he said when entering Madinah, narrated by Abdullah Bin Salam, "...The first thing he said was,

"O people, spread (the greeting of) Salam, offer food to people and pray at night when people are sleeping, you will enter Paradise in peace." [Sunan Ibn Majah]

I spread peace by saying Salam to people I see, and by doing nice things to them that put them at ease.

There were six neighbors of the Prophet (SAWS), five of them used to throw trash on him, but the story only mentions one neighbor doing it. When they threw trash, the Prophet (SAWS) would pick it up with a stick, and say, "O Bani Abd Manaf, what kind of neighborly treatment is this?" Then he would throw it on the street. [Ibn Hisham 1:416]

At home, my brother sometimes gets on my nerves, and I ignore him instead of saying anything back, like the Prophet (SAWS) and those neighbors.

The Prophet (SAWS) did not lift a hand in retribution against these people, showing us how peaceful he was, to have camel guts thrown on him and not fling them back! Here are some examples of his justness:

Abdullah Ibn Sahl (RA) and his cousin, Mahisah (RA), were appointed to collect rent from the Jews of Khaybar, but on the way, they separated. Abdullah (RA) was waylaid and killed, and Mahisah (RA) reported this tragedy. Since there were no eyewitnesses against the Jews, Muhammad (SAWS) paid the blood money out of state revenues. *[Sahih Al-Bukhari]*

A woman of the Makhzoom family, a family with good connections, was found guilty of theft. Some people intervened to save her, but Prophet Muhammad (SAWS) said,

"Many a community ruined itself in the past, as they only punished the poor and ignored the offenses of the exalted. By Allah, if Muhammad's daughter Fatimah would have committed theft, her hand would have been severed." [Sahih Al-Bukhari]

At school, there was a contest about who would be captains in basketball, and I was watching, so they asked me to say who won, and even though I knew that the loser would be a better captain, I told them who rightfully won, just like the Prophet (SAWS) and that lady.

Once, the Prophet (SAWS) was distributing war booty, and the people were flocking around him. One man fell upon him, and Muhammad (SAWS) pushed him with a stick, causing a slight abrasion. He was so sorry about this that he told the man he could have revenge. He said,

"O Prophet of Allah, I forgive you." [Sunan Abi Dawud]

This shows that we should not have any bias against or for anybody when it comes to justice.

Abu Hurayrah (RA) narrated that the Prophet (SAWS) said,

"...removing harmful things from the road is a charity." [Sahih Al-Bukhari]

Once, I went with my Boy Scout troop to clean a stream. It was littered with plastics and other materials. We cleaned it, and it was flowing smoothly again. That is justice to nature and the community.

These are the definitions of peace, justice, and the Prophet's (SAWS) teachings, and how I implement them in my daily life.

2nd Place: Jenna Awadallah
Al-Rahmah School, Baltimore, MD

"A Moment of Justice is Better than a Year of Worship"

-Prophet Muhammad (SAWS) [Sunan Ibn Majah]

The way I stay peaceful and just in my daily life is through the remembrance of Allah. Allah is As- Salaam which means the giver of peace. Throughout my day I always try to remember Allah in everything I do. In Surah Al-Ra'd, Allah (SWT) says,

"Unquestionably, by the remembrance of Allah hearts are assured." [Al-Quran; 13:28]

Whenever I feel frustrated or overwhelmed, I remind myself that Allah is always with me and He will ease my task for me, InshaAllah. Allah (SWT) says in Surah Al-Hadid,

"...and He is with you wherever you are..." [Al-Quran; 57:4]

Remembering Allah and putting my trust in Him helps me stay peaceful and just throughout my day. Justice is also a very important aspect of Islam. Allah (SWT) says in Surah Al-Anaam,

"...And when you testify, be just..." [Al-Quran; 6:152]

However, sometimes it can be difficult to be just. Whenever I am in a conflict or difficult situation, I remember Ayah 135 in Surah An-Nisaa,

"O you who have believed, be persistently standing firm in justice, witnesses for Allah, even if it be against yourselves or parents and relatives." [Al-Quran; 4:135]

This Ayah reminds me how much importance Allah has placed on being just, so I always try my very best to be just and fair in all I do. Even if someone is unjust to me, I try to remember that Allah is the most just and will help me deal with injustice. I like to make the dua:

"Allah is sufficient as our helper and Allah is the best of protectors."

Another way I remember to stay peaceful and just, is by remembering the examples of Prophet Muhammed (SAWS). Our Prophet (SAWS) was always at peace even when faced with difficulty and he always served justly no matter what the situation. The Prophet Muhammed (SAWS) is an inspiration to me and reminds me that if I follow Allah's path and do good deeds, InshaAllah, I will always be able to maintain peace and justice in my daily life. Abdullah Ibn Salaam (RA) narrated that the Prophet Muhammed (SAWS) said,

"O people! Spread (the greeting of) Salam, feed others, uphold the ties of kinship, and pray during the night when people are sleeping, and you will enter Paradise with Salam." [Sunan Ibn Majah]

This hadith testifies to the peaceful nature of the Prophet (SAWS) because the narrator of this hadith, Abdullah Ibn Salaam, was a Jewish Rabbi at the time. When he went to meet the Prophet (SAWS) the first thing he heard him say was this hadith and it left a lasting impression on him, and he became Muslim. SubhanAllah. I try my best to spread peace and follow the way of the Prophet (SAWS).

3rd Place: Iman Neja
Al-Huda School, College Park, MD

"There is nothing heavier than good character put in the scale of a believer on the Day of Resurrection." -Prophet Muhammed [Sunan Abi Dawud]

Your character is part of you, and your character depends on your ability to be peaceful and just when you go about your daily life. Today, as we go about our daily lives, it often becomes difficult to stay peaceful and be just with those around us. Especially in this day and age, when people brand Islam as a violent and unjust religion. Islam is of a peaceful nature and teaches us to be just in our dealings. It is simple to stay peaceful and adhere to justice in our daily lives.

First, we must understand what it means to be peaceful. To be peaceful means that you have rid yourself of the ruinations of the heart. Examples of these ruinations that are around today are war, hate, and violence. It's a thing that one sees every day on the news, right? Turn on channel so and so, and we see news about possible war or a hate crime that has occurred. Then, we must understand what it means to be just. To be just means that you have made a decision based on facts and not empty opinion. You see that every day. Every day we see decisions made because of favoritism or relationships. For example, a judge from Canada might pick Canadians. As a Muslim, it is easy to see that being violent and unjust will lead to corruption.

Allah tells us in the Quran,

"The believers are but brothers, so make settlement between your brothers. And fear Allah that you may receive mercy." [Al-Quran, 49:10]

Allah is telling us, as Muslims, to make peace with the rest of humanity for we are all brothers. How different is that from the claim that Muslims are terrorists! Nowadays, people who are violent and unjust publicize it as cool. Screaming at your waiter has become a fad now. The Prophet Muhammad (SAWS) once assisted a woman who had never met him before and didn't recognize him as the prophet. She spoke of the Prophet and was insulting him. When Prophet Muhammad finished helping her, she asked his name and he introduced himself. She was shocked because of his peacefulness. She had expected him to be violent, especially after her insults. See how the Prophet (SAWS) maintained peace in his dealings? We can too!

Peace and justice are like the wings of a bird, without one wing, the bird is not complete. Likewise, without peace, your character is not complete. It's the same the other way around. If we do not attain peace and justice, we risk hellfire- the worst possible punishment. We, as Muslims, can confront violence, hatred, and injustice. We must do the opposite. We cannot hate the haters. If we do, we have failed. We confront violence with peace, hate with love, and injustice with justice.

What makes it simple to stay peaceful and adhere to justice are three main components: understanding it, having examples to follow, and implementing it. First, we must understand what peace and justice is. Then, we must see the best of all examples the Prophet (SAWS) and his companions (RA). Lastly, we must know how to act in the way of peace and justice. We, the Muslims, have the best gift that any nation could have- we hold the key to peace and justice. That's what makes us incredible.

HIGH SCHOOL | LEVEL 6

Topic:

How does the Prophet's (SAWS) teachings bring peace and justice and how would you implement those to our lives and communities today? What would be your role to inform the community and society about the role of Islam in establishing peace and justice in the society at large? What actions can you take individually and collectively?

1st Place: Emira-Syeda Ali
Home School, Gaithersburg, MD

Islam is our way of life, and it describes all of our behavior. No action direct or indirect, transparent or subtle, can be separated from the practice of our deen. So, what is the source of our deen, adab, and akhlaq? It is the kalimatullah of the Qur'an and the sayings and teachings of RasulAllah (SAWS). Since the Qur'an contains Allah's words, the relevance in our lives needs no further explanation. The Sunnah of our beloved Prophet (SAWS) is as relevant today as they were during the lifetime of the Prophet (SAWS). The Qur'an and Sunnah should be viewed as one as you cannot separate one from the other. Sa'd bin Hisham Ibn Amir reported:

I said to Aisha (RA), "Ya Ummul-Mu'minin, tell me about the character of RasulAllah (SAWS)." Aisha (RA) said, "Have you not read the Qur'an?" I said, "Of course." Aisha (RA) said, "Verily, the character of RasulAllah (SAWS) was the Qur'an...." [Sahih Muslim]

Peace and justice are overriding concepts in Islam, and they permeate our actions. Sometimes we tend to forget about the simple things that we need to establish a just and peaceful world. First and foremost, individually and collectively as a society, we need to improve how we interact and relate to one another. The origin of conflict appears to be complicated, but the root causes are often simple. This means that from the moment we encounter someone to the moment we leave someone's company we behave in a polite and appropriate manner. Abdullah Ibn Amr (RA) reported that RasulAllah (SAWS) said:

"Whoever would love to be delivered from Hellfire and admitted into Paradise, let him meet his end with faith in Allah (SWT) and the Last Day, and let him treat people as he would love to be treated." [Sahih Muslim]

What comes next is the context of our speech and the manner in which we speak. We must avoid vain speech and backbiting. On the surface this appears benign, but often it is the seemingly innocuous backbiting that leads to larger conflicts. Allah (SWT) says in the Qur'an:

"...And do not spy, nor backbite one another. Would any of you like to eat the flesh of their dead brother? You would despise that!" [Al-Quran; 49:12]

Often, our conversations often start off fine, but they easily digress in a bad direction. The challenge is trying to change the course of the conversation if possible or leaving the conversation altogether. If we do not avoid backbiting, there will be consequences. Anas (RA) narrated that RasulAllah (SAWS) said,

"During the Mi'raj, I saw a group of people who were scratching their chests and faces with their copper nails. I asked, 'Who are these people, O Jibreel?' Jibreel (AS) replied: 'These are the people who ate flesh of others (by backbiting) and trampled people's honor.'" [Sunan Abi Dawud]

When talking to someone, we need the virtue of patience. In this era of instant gratification, it seems counter-intuitive to say that patience is a virtue. But the Qur'an and the Sunnah emphasize the need for patience in the face of adverse challenging conditions.

Abu-Huraira (RA) narrated that RasulAllah (SAWS) said:

"The example of a believer is that of a fresh tender plant; from whatever direction the wind comes, it bends it, but when the wind becomes quiet, it becomes straight again. Similarly, a believer is afflicted with calamities (but he remains patient till Allah removes his difficulties.) And an impious wicked person is like a pine tree which keeps hard

and straight till Allah cuts (breaks) it down when He wishes." [Sahih Al-Bukhari]

Let us look at a famous example from our Prophet (SAWS) to get a better perspective on patience. When we look at the incident of Ta'if, our Prophet (SAWS) was fiercely attacked by the enemies of Islam, and then Allah sent Jibreel (AS), and the Angel of the Mountains, to our Prophet (SAWS), asking him if he wanted these people to be punished by destructing their entire town. Let us think about that for a moment in the context of today's world. Today, we are quick to ostracize and seek to avenge every perceived wrong committed against the Ummah. Here, we have a clear example of people who deserved some sort of punishment for their actions. Instead, while the Prophet was sitting in his blood-soaked shoes and presented with the option of punishing the people, he chose to forgive them and make dua that they accept Islam. If the punishment was implemented, it would have destroyed people who were not yet Muslim. It is hard to imagine a world without Ta'if today. It is a thriving, predominantly Muslim city and a popular tourist and vacation spot for Muslim tourists.

In conclusion, we have all of the information we need in the Qur'an and the Sunnah of our beloved Prophet (SAWS) to establish a just and peaceful society. We explored a few basic things we can implement in our daily lives. These ideas are practical and can be implemented by all of us with some minimal effort, but it will have maximum impact. Islam is easy and if we actually implement our faith in our daily lives, we will easily promote peace and justice. The purpose of life is to achieve real happiness by worshiping the one true Allah in everything we do. Allah (SWT) says in the Qur'an:

"O believers! Stand firm for Allah and bear true testimony. Do not let the hatred of a people lead you to injustice. Be just! That is closer to righteousness..." [Al-Qur'an; 5:8]

Before I finish my essay, I will leave you with one question, to ponder upon: do you not want to strive to attain peace and justice in this world? I ask Allah (SWT) to make it easy for all of us, to take the right action to promote peace and justice, and also make it easy for us to follow the footsteps of our beloved Prophet (SAWS). Allahumma-Ameen!

2nd Place: Musa Ahmad
Homeschool, Lanham, MD

Allah says in the Quran,

"Indeed, in the Messenger of Allah you have an excellent example for whoever has hope in Allah and the Last Day and remembers Allah often." [Al-Quran; 33:21]

We can learn how to implement peace and justice in our communities from the teachings of the Prophet (SAWS), but more so from his actions. Makkah was filled with injustice, and Madinah was engulfed in war and hatred. The Prophet (SAWS) brought justice to Makkah and brought peace to Madinah. We can learn from his example and implement his teachings in our world today. There are many problems around us for which we can find solutions in the teachings and actions of the Prophet (SAWS). In this essay, I will be highlighting three problems, namely racism, economic inequality, and mental health issues, which in my opinion, are the root cause of injustice and conflict in our communities today.

In our communities, we often see racism and discrimination against African Americans. One of the main reasons African Americans are stereotyped is because of the way slavery was introduced and later abolished in the United States. One day a man was a slave, and the next day he was free. On the surface, this may look like a good thing but, in reality, this was a catastrophe. This way of abolition left many African Americans homeless and jobless. Many went hungry and suffered greatly, which in some instances increased the crime among these communities. However, when we look at how Islam abolished slavery, we can see how the teachings of the Prophet (SAWS) and how he dealt with it, differed from the way our predecessors dealt with it here in the United States. Instead of forbidding slavery instantly, he set down rules and regulations, which eventually led to the eradication of slavery. The Prophet (SAWS) said,

"Your slaves are your brethren upon whom Allah has given you authority. So, if one has one's brethren under one's control, one should feed them with the like of what one eats and clothe them with the like of what one wears. You should not overburden them with what they cannot bear, and if you do so, help them (in their hard job)." [Sahih al-Bukhari]

Economic inequality is growing rapidly in the United States and around the world. The rich are getting richer, and the poor are getting poorer. One of the main reasons for this is because the rich are not taking care of the poor. Many times, even the government officials are funded by the rich, which causes government decisions to be in their favor. There is also no interaction between the rich and poor in our communities and our economic status determines who we are in society. However, at the time of the Prophet (SAWS), we have many examples of sahabah who were less fortunate that were good friends with other rich sahabah and interacted with them daily. This breaks the barrier between economic classes and builds empathy, which leads to the rich assisting the less fortunate. Islam makes zakah obligatory and strongly encourages giving charity. According to a study done by The Guardian in 2017, if all Muslims pay zakah, poverty would be eradicated in the world. This only includes the 1.8 billion Muslims in the world, let alone the other six billion people. This is yet another example of how if we implement the teachings of the Prophet (SAWS) in our society today, it will bring justice not only to the Muslims but to humanity at large.

"Unquestionably in the remembrance of Allah the hearts are assured. " [Al-Quran; 13:28]

In today's world, most people believe that they can attain happiness through money, power, fame, and other worldly pleasures.

This ideology leads many people to depression and other mental health issues. Some people who don't have these worldly pleasures get depressed because they feel that if they did, they would attain happiness when the fact is that many of those who have achieved excessive amounts of wealth and fame realize that these things did not bring them happiness. That's why we see many celebrities on anti-depressants and committing suicide. Statistics show that as of 2019 approximately 300 million people are going through depression worldwide. Depression is an epidemic that is growing rapidly in today's society. The Prophet (SAWS) said,

"Look at those who are lower than you (financially) but do not look at those who are higher than you, lest you belittle the favors Allah conferred upon you." [Bulugh al Maram]

He also taught us that,

"Whoever makes the hereafter his goal, Allah makes his heart rich and organizes his affairs, and the world comes to him whether it wants to or not. And whoever makes the world his goal, Allah puts his poverty right before his eyes and disorganizes his affairs, and the world does not come to him, except what has been decreed for him." [Sunan At-Tirmidhi]

If we follow the teachings and advice of the Prophet (SAWS), this will help us be satisfied and grateful for what we have and bring peace within ourselves and, in turn, to our communities as a whole.

In this essay, I have identified three key problems and shown how the example of the Prophet (SAWS) will help resolve these issues. One of the main reasons for racism in America is slavery. If we had followed the example of the Prophet (SAWS), slavery wouldn't have been the way it was, and it wouldn't have ended the way it did. The practice of giving and taking care of the less fortunate and needy, as taught by the Prophet (SAWS), can help bridge the gap of economic inequality and consequently eradicate poverty.

If we base our lives on the remembrance of Allah and the hereafter, we would be satisfied with our lives, and depression would be at much lower levels then it is today. In conclusion, we need to implement the teachings of the Prophet (SAWS) by following his example to bring about peace and justice in our communities.

3rd Place: Muhammad Islam
ERH, Fulton, MD

Prophet Muhammad's (SAWS) teachings would bring justice and peace to our lives and communities today by making us realize their importance and encouraging us to take actions that will ensure justice and peace are brought.

The Messenger (SAWS)'s teachings highlight how crucial justice and peace is in our lives and communities today. As narrated in a hadith by Abu Huraira (RA), the Messenger of Allah (SAWS) said:

"You will not enter Paradise until you believe, and you will not believe until you love each other. Shall I show you something that, if you did, you would love each other? Spread peace among yourselves." [Sahih Muslim]

In other words, in order for us to enter Paradise, the ultimate goal of any Muslim, we need to spread peace in our communities during our lives. If we don't try to spread peace, however, we will not be able to enter Paradise and thereby drop ourselves into the Blazing Fire. The Prophet (SAWS) also highlights the importance of justice in our lives and community. He told us that if we *"establish justice"* in our community, we will get *"a sadaqa (charitable gift) ... for every joint of [our] human [bodies]"* and everyday there will be *"a reward of a sadaqa"* [Sahih Bukhari] Therefore, our Prophet (SAWS)'s teachings show the extreme importance of bringing justice and peace in our lives and communities today.

But what can I do to spread peace in our lives and communities today? Well, one of the actions that I can do, individually, is to stay happy by being thankful for everything that I have.

Our Prophet (SAWS)'s teachings tell us that if we truly are believers, then *"there is good for [us] in everything"* because when we face happy, joyful times, we *"[express] gratitude to Allah"* and when we face painful times, we *"[endure] it patiently"* [Sahih Muslim] By staying happy with our possessions, we prevent conflicts to build up within our communities, leaving it at peace.

Another action that I could do is to help others in our communities. According to Abu Hurairah (RA), the Prophet (SAWS) once said that,

"He who alleviates the suffering of a brother out of the sufferings of the world, Allah would alleviate his suffering from the sufferings of the Day of Resurrection, and he who finds relief for one who is hard-pressed, Allah would make things easy for him in the Hereafter" [Sahih Muslim]

This shows us that by helping others, we will have an easier Hereafter. This thought should make us happier and, in turn, have peace in our lives. Not only that, by helping others, we strengthen relationships with others more, making them harder to break and harder to cause conflict, but easier to have peace.

The most challenging yet imperative action that I could do that will require a collective effort is to prevent nonviolence from occurring in our lives and in our communities. Our beloved Messenger (SAWS) taught us that *"[t]here should be neither harming"* or hurting others, nor should there be *"reciprocating harm"* or hurting ourselves [Sunan Ibn Majah]. This allows our communities to be unharmed and our lives to be unharmed, leading to peace. To follow this hadith, we have to be friendly with one another and help each other so that we aren't as likely to be bitter. I should try to gather everyone in our communities as frequently as possible and get to know each other better, making it easier to determine whether anyone is having a bad time or a bad relationship.

If someone is in such a bad situation, I should help them out so that they don't start acting fierce. If I do see Muslims from our communities start acting violently, as seen currently on various parts of the globe, I should try to condemn it and stop it using whatever means by leading everyone.

There are other actions to take to ensure peace that can't be covered here due to the limited scope of this essay. But there are also as many actions to establish justice in our communities and lives. One action, that is raising a lot of attention in our society, is to oppose discrimination. The Prophet (SAWS) once was asked about who is *"the most honorable...in Allah's sight"*, specifically about "the virtues of the ancestry of the Arabs" to which he replied that

"The best amongst you in the Pre-Islamic Period are the best among you in Islam if they comprehend (Islam)." [Sahih Bukhari]

This meant that our Prophet (SAWS) taught in his teachings that we can only rank people in our communities based off how they practice Islam, both externally and internally. Since there's no way for us to judge that, we as Muslims have no absolute reason to discriminate within ourselves. We should, therefore, prevent discrimination in our society to the best of our ability. This could be done collectively, as I or anyone could gather as many Muslims in our communities as possible and prevent any discriminatory act from happening that is currently happening. In the U.S, for example, this could be done by lobbying Congress whenever we see a discriminatory act, like Executive Order 13769 that banned Muslim entry, to pass legislation that opposes such an act.

I will also need to act against and prevent oppression in our communities and our lives. Anas (RA) narrated:

The Messenger of Allah (SAWS) said: "Help your brother whether he is an oppressor or an oppressed," A man said, "O Allah's Messenger

(SAWS)! I will help him if he is oppressed, but if he is an oppressor, how shall I help him?" The Prophet (SAWS) said, *"By preventing him from oppressing (others), for that is how to help him."* [Sahih al-Bukhari]

This obligates me to take measures to oppose oppression by informing others about such acts so all of us in our communities could take action.

Hence, peace and justice are highly emphasized by the Prophet (SAWS). There are many actions I can do to ensure them and inform about them in our communities and our lives.

2021

Navigating the Covid-19 Pandemic

MAFIQ FOUNDATION PRESENTS EPC 2021

ISLAM AS A SPIRITUAL CURE: NAVIGATING THE COVID-19 PANDEMIC

SATURDAY • JANUARY 23, 2021
VIA ZOOM

SUBMISSION DEADLINE: JANUARY 10

ELEMENTARY SCHOOL
Name some blessings your family has had in spite of the lockdown and not being able to do all of the normal day-to-day things done before the pandemic.

MIDDLE SCHOOL
Describe how Muslims have been using their faith and teachings of the Prophet Muhammad (S) to positively impact their communities even when they are facing hardships.

HIGH SCHOOL
Some say the coronavirus pandemic is a punishment, some say it is a test. Either way, what should the mindset of a Muslim be during a global event of this scale and how should that translate into productive action?

MORE INFORMATION:
epc.mafiq.org

CONTACT
essays@mafiq.org

A platform for the Muslim youth to foster their communication skills

ELEMENTARY SCHOOL | LEVEL 1

Topic:

Write a letter to someone telling them about the blessings your family has had during this pandemic.

This poster was submitted by Merium Ahmed of Level 1.

Young Muslim Voices

1st Place: Zaynab Mehmood
MCC, Silver Spring, MD

Dear Abbu,

Assalamualaikum! I hope you are doing well and are staying safe. The COVID-19 pandemic has been a scary and confusing time. It has been one year since I have hugged you. This year was filled with sadness, but there were some blessings as well. My mom taught me that Allah (SWT) says in the Quran:

"So, surely with hardship comes ease." [Al-Quran; 94:5]

I believe that Allah (SWT) will give us an easy time soon. In the meantime, I learned that I have three blessings that I can juggle! The first blessing is the Quran and dhikr. The second is food and safety. The third blessing ball is fun!

Blessing ball number 1 is very special to me. It is the Quran and dhikr. I have memorized four new surah. I am also reading my Nooraniyyah in the mornings. My siblings and I are learning new dhikr. The Prophet (SAWS) said,

"(The following are) two words (sentences or utterances) that are very easy for the tongue to say, and very heavy in the balance (of reward), and most beloved to the Gracious Almighty (And they are): Subhan Allahi wa bi- hamdihi; Subhan Allahi-l-'Adhim" [Sahih Al-Bukhari]

Blessing ball number is 2 is food and safety. I have to wear my COVID-19 mask and gloves to juggle this ball! I learned how to make sushi and brownies. I feel blessed to stay home and be safe from COVID-19. My Dad got the vaccine, alhamdulillah!

My last juggling ball is fun! We went into nature a lot during 2020. We went to the beaches in MD/VA. We went camping at Assateague Island and my living room. We saw a lot of horses on the island. My family played a lot of board games like Clue, Monopoly, and Risk. We got pet goldfish and now they are huge! We played in the pool and had water balloon fights. We explored new places like Liberty Dam, Shenandoah, Great Falls and many farms.

Abbu, I hope you have seen my three juggling blessing balls. COVID-19 has been hard but also easy. Allah (SWT) loves you and me. I cannot wait to hug you in 2021!

Much love,
Your grandchild

2nd Place: Raidah Islam
Al-Huda School, College Park, MD

Assalamu Alaikum Danya Api,

How are you? Alhamdulillah, I am fine. I learned from my mom that coronavirus is dangerous because it can spread from one person to another. It makes us sick which does not allow us to go near people. I cannot go to school, play with my friends, or go to the playground. Everyone needs to wear a mask now. Before the coronavirus, I used to go swimming but now I can't go. But even after all of this, I still feel blessed by Allah for many reasons. So, I am writing this letter to tell you about some of the blessings that I have experienced during this pandemic.

First of all, I am blessed that I can spend time with my family. I feel safe around them. I like talking and playing with them. Do you remember when my parents got sick? I was sad because I couldn't go close to them. It's a blessing from Allah that they are not sick anymore and I can play with them again.

My next blessing is Zoom because I can see my teachers and friends there. I don't have to wake up early in the morning to get ready for school. I don't have to wear my uniform and I have less school time. I also have art classes through Zoom, and we have so much fun. Another blessing is the nature that Allah created. For example, the sun and the trees. The sun gives us warmth and light. Trees give us oxygen that we breathe. But, thanks to Allah, I am healthy and safe.

So, Danya Api Covid 19 is hard but there are so many blessings that come from it.

Love XX

3rd Place: Alisha Memon
Al-Fatih Academy, Reston, VA

Dear Muhammad (SAW),

Assalamualaikum Warahmatullahi Wabarakatuh

I have learned many things from your teachings through Hadiths, books about you, your companions, stories of your characteristics, and through Shamail. You have passed on the Quran to us. All of that taught me how to be grateful in any situation. I think that if you had not taught me how to be patient, this situation of COVID pandemic would be very different and even more difficult than how it is at this moment. But there are a lot of things I am grateful for. School starts later and ends earlier so I have gotten more and more time to do the things I enjoy doing by myself and doing things with family. I am also very grateful to Allah for keeping our health at a good level. I am happy that we have a spacious and comfortable home, good food and clean water. Below are some more things I am grateful for.

1. Fasting during Ramadan because school was shorter, preparing and doing Iftar and Suhoor together.
2. Being able to take many different online classes from the comfort of my home.
3. Watching live shows, read-alouds and plays even when they are in different states or countries.
4. Praying taraweeh every night because school started later each day.
5. Getting to do a lot of fun things with my parents and older sister.
6. We started doing a Family Fun Day aka FFD once a month where none of us would do any work but play and do activities altogether. We did a family cook-off, hikes, scavenger hunts in

the neighborhood, art workshops, photo competitions, building projects etc.
7. Watching 'Angels in your Presence' each night of Ramadan with the family and learning many interesting facts about angels.
8. I baked tons of new recipes like cupcakes, cakes, cookies, etc. with my family or by myself with their help.

You taught me to look to the good side instead of the bad side. I learned from you that even if there are a lot of bad things going on you still focus on the good things that are going on. This pandemic has been very difficult as we do not get to do things as we normally would do. But I know that Allah made this trial happen for a reason and at some point, it will get better. I am very thankful to have guidance from you in different forms.

Signed, XX

Special Recognition – Essay: Dua Syed
ADAMS Center, Sterling, VA

Dear Sofia, Assalamu Alaikum,

Allah (SWT) says in Surah Ibrahim,

"And remember when your Lord proclaimed, 'If you are grateful, I will certainly give you more. But if you are ungrateful, surely My punishment is severe.'" [Al-Quran; 14:7]

It is very important for Muslims to be thankful. Sometimes, when we are focusing on the hardships and tests in life, we forget about all the good things Allah (SWT) has blessed us with. The pandemic has been a very scary and sad time. In spite of the lockdown, my family has had many blessings. We are thankful for these blessings. Some of these blessings are each other, food, water, masks, soap, doctors and hospitals, medicines, phones, and computers.

The first blessing my family has had throughout the pandemic is each other. During the pandemic, I have been blessed to be able to stay at home with my family. The time we spend together keeps me happy and calm, despite all the changes in the world around us. Another blessing we have is food and water. We have masks to protect ourselves and others when we go out. We are able to use soap to wash our hands. We also live in an area where there are hospitals and doctors' offices nearby. There are also stores near me that have medicines. We are thankful for phones that let us talk to our family and friends. Another blessing we have are computers, which we use to go to school online.

Throughout the pandemic, I often think about how the Prophets of the past dealt with tests and challenges. For example, how Prophet Yunus (AS) turned to Allah (SWT) from the stomach of a whale.

Or, how the Prophet Ibrahim (AS) had to leave his wife and baby in the middle of the desert, with full faith in Allah (SWT). And how the Prophet Muhammad (SAWS), despite the mistreatment from the disbelievers, continued to spread Islam. What I learn from these stories is how no test is too hard for me to handle. If Allah (SWT) tests me, I know He knows I am strong enough, smart enough, and brave enough to handle it.

Even with all the sadness and fear during the pandemic, I have many blessings to be thankful for. Allah (SWT) wants the Muslims to be grateful, even when times are hard. I thank Allah (SWT) for not testing me with difficulties as challenging as those he tested the many Prophets with. During the pandemic, I will continue to remember the blessings my family and I have and thank Allah (SWT) each day.

May Allah (SWT) help us feel calm and at peace, even with all of the difficulties around us. May He bless us with strength and bravery to face these hard times. May Allah (SWT) keep us and everyone in the world in good health. May He end the pandemic. May Allah (SWT) help us stay grateful throughout our lives.

Love,
Your best friend

Special Recognition – Speech: Bilal Gbadamosi
Home School, Lanham, MD

Dear Isa,

Assalaam alaykum. How are you and your family? I hope you are all doing well. This past year has been hard, boring, and stressful for most families but alhamdulillah it hasn't been that bad during this pandemic and my family have had a lot of blessings during COVID-19.

We are grateful to Allah for keeping us in good health and not letting us catch the virus. We've been doing a lot of activities together. At home we do family halaqah (taleem), reading Quran, praying, and playing. I also help my mom bake. Outside, me and my family walt at the park on the trail and around the lake. We also went to an aquarium and saw so many underwater creatures. I also had playdates with another friend. These are the fun things I got to do online. These are the classes I did like kids Seerah Intensive, Names of Allah, Stories from Surah Al-Kahf, cooking class, sahabah series, cub scout, art class, and a lot more. I am also working on a COVID time capsule.

For Ramadan, we prayed taraweeh and had suhoor and iftar together. We got to go for some drive through iftars. Eid was also great! We did a drive through Eid prayer and parties! I got goodie bags! I also helped my family with organizing for our masjid.

I have had a lot of fun and they have been amazing blessings! I hope you also had a lot of fun with your family. Please write back and tell me about it.

Your friend.

ELEMENTARY SCHOOL | LEVEL 2

Topic:

Muslims have faced many challenges in their daily lives due to the coronavirus pandemic, however, many blessings have come from this as well. Name some blessings your family has had in spite of the lockdown and not being able to do all of the normal day-to-day things you would do before the pandemic.

Image from: https://qute-coloring-pages.com/coloring/train-drawing-for-kids-9.html

Young Muslim Voices

1st Place: Musa Rahmani
Washington International Academy, Alexandria, VA

It was a typical day of school for me. I studied hard, had fun with my friends, and thought that the next day would be the same. But later, I learned that no one would be going to school for a few days. Then, a few days became many more days, and those days became weeks. We switched to online learning and then every day, the world changed. A virus called the coronavirus had struck the world and we couldn't go outside, go to school, or do any of our normal day-to-day activities. However, despite all of the challenges I have experienced this year, there are many blessings I have that I always try to remember and be grateful for.

For the past year, I have learned that millions of people around the world have become sick and have died. Sometimes, when I am about to complain about not being able to go to school or do normal activities, I remember the challenges that people are experiencing. This makes me realize what is truly important and helps me count the many blessings that I have. I am grateful for my health, my family, my home, and the ability to have healthy food and to gain an education. I can breathe clean air, drink clean water and eat healthy food that my mom prepares for me without any difficulty, and have a warm and happy home that my family and I live in, Alhamdulilah. Above all, the most important blessing that I have is Islam. As a Muslim, I believe being grateful and patient is the key to getting through challenges. Allah (SWT) has told us,

"We will certainly test you with a touch of fear and famine and loss of property, life, and crops. Give good news to those who patiently endure— who, when faced with a disaster, say, "Surely to Allah we belong and to Him we will all return." They are the ones who will receive Allah's blessings and mercy. And it is they who are rightly guided."

[Al-Quran; 2:155-157]

There are also many stories from the Prophets that teach us the importance of remaining patient. The Prophet Ayyub (AS) was a very blessed man, but Allah (SWT) willed that he should experience many trials. He became very sick, lost many of his family members, and his wealth. He never gave up his trust in Allah (SWT) and remained patient. He thought about all that Allah (SWT) had given him and what he still had despite what he was facing. These tests allowed him to pray more and increase his faith. Soon, Allah (SWT) gave him a fountain that cured his illnesses. During the past year, I have learned this story and others, which has taught me about the importance of remaining patient, being grateful for the blessings that I have, and always holding a strong belief that Allah (SWT) is in charge of everything. I pray that these difficult times make us better Muslims with stronger Emaan, inshallah!

Young Muslim Voices

2nd Place: Hamza- Syed Ali
Home School, Gaithersburg, MD

It is true that the pandemic has troubled us. At the same time, it is true the pandemic has many blessings. Yes, it is different, but my family and I are enjoying the blessings. I still miss the things we used to do before COVID-19, but we found fun ways to spend our time.

I live close to our Masjid and before the pandemic we went there every day. We rarely prayed together at home since we went to the Masjid. When the Masjid closed, we missed praying in Jama'at. My sister had the idea that we try to pray in Jama'at. Then we started to pray all the Salat together, Alhamdulilah. Ibn Umar (RA) said, Rasulullah (SAWS) said:

"Salat in congregation is twenty-seven degrees more virtuous than a man's Salat alone." [Sunan At-Tirmidhi]

Last Ramadan, Masajids were closed. All the things we did at the Masjid during Ramadan we did it at home. The coolest thing we did was praying Taraweeh together and completely reciting the Qur'an. The reward for reading the Qur'an is humongous. RasulAllah (SAWS) said:

"[Whoever recites a letter] from Allah's Book, then he receives the reward from it, and the reward of ten the like of it. I do not say that Alif-Lam-Mim is a letter, but Alif is a letter, Lam is a letter and Mim is a letter'" [Sunan At-Tirmidhi]

Before COVID-19, we saw my uncle, aunt, and cousins at the Masjid although they live nearby. We created a small bubble to see each other. We go to my cousins' house on Fridays. My aunt makes yummy food for us.

After we eat, we watch cartoons, then we play fun games. On Saturdays, they come to our house. I help my family by working to clean our house. We talk about football and play games, and we try a new dessert every week. On Sundays, I watch football with my family. Alhamdulilah, since the pandemic we have had even more fun together. AbuHurayrah (RA) reported that RasulAllah (SAWS) said,

'...he who believes in Allah and the Last Day, let him maintain good the ties of blood relationship" [Sahih Al- Bukhari]

Before COVID-19, I wasted my free time by doing nothing. After the pandemic I realized time is important and I need to use it wisely. Alhamdulilah, I spend my free time learning about Islam. I started to listen to Islamic lectures for children. I learned about the prophets and some Sahabas. I joined an online class where we learn about Islamic manners. I sit with my family when they are watching Islamic lectures from different scholars. Anas (RA) narrated that Rasulullah (SAWS) said:

"Seeking knowledge is a duty upon every Muslim..." [Sunan Ibn Majah]

In conclusion, there are many challenges in the pandemic, but many blessings and interesting things came during this pandemic. We prayed together and we read the entire Qur'an together. We learned to spend time with our family and enjoy it. I am able to learn about Islam by listening to lectures. Insha'Allah I hope we learned some good habits that we will continue once the pandemic is over.

Young Muslim Voices

3rd Place: Eliza Khan
Nova Elm Academy, Sterling, VA

Despite the coronavirus being so small in size, it has changed everyone's life in some way. Many people see this virus as a calamity, but we can look at it as a blessing in disguise. The COVID-19 pandemic has created a lot of tragedy in several different ways, but it has brought some blessings such as increased family time, learning not to take things for granted, and finding more about my hobbies. Allah says,

"Perhaps you dislike something which is good for you and like something which is bad for you. Allah knows and you do not know." [Al-Quran; 2:216]

Many of us do not like this virus, but it may be something good for us that we do not like. The first blessing of the coronavirus is that I am able to spend so much more time with my family. Before the pandemic, we were always busy going to school and many places that we rarely had quality family time. Now I can play games with my siblings, enjoy a family dinner, and most importantly, we have added a new addition to our family: our new kitten. We never thought that we would get a kitten, but Allah has blessed us in ways we had never imagined. I have learned to appreciate Allah's blessings and to not take our simple daily actions for granted. From as simple as going to school to going to the masjid, everything is closed, but at the end of the day, I see this as a gift from Allah because I have more free time on my hands.

The second blessing of the coronavirus is that I am able to find and discover my hobbies. Because of the free time I have, I started to improve my creativity and artistic skills, gymnastics, painting, as well as cooking with my mom. I discovered a new passion for cooking that I never thought I had. I learned how to cook my cultural food and realized how fun it is to make and delicious to eat. After I cook, I have such a rewarding feeling that makes me feel proud of myself that I accomplished such a task. Along with cooking, I have become better at cleaning my room. Doing my own chores makes me realize how hard my mom works.

All the teachings of the Prophet (SAWS) that he taught us over 1400 years ago are coming back. People are starting to realize staying clean, avoiding shaking hands, and even wearing the niqab (face covering) is an important mechanism for keeping us safe. In fact, the Prophet (SAWS) said, *"Cleanliness is half of faith..." [Sahih Muslim]*

Many people across the nation are suffering from this virus and have even passed away. Above all, we should thank Allah that he has given us another chance to do more good deeds. In addition to this, the virus teaches us to have patience in Allah's plan because He is the best of planners.

Special Recognition – Essay: Airo Keri
Al-Huda School, College Park, MD

Many changes have been made ever since Covid-19 hit. We have been quarantining in our houses and have been living our lives differently. Despite that fact, we should look at the bright side. You will notice that there are many blessings and mercies from Allah. These blessings have also brought us closer to Allah. Three things that we have been blessed with during these hard times are being clean, online education, and spending time with our family.

Being clean is something that everyone is trying to do. Due to how easily corona spreads, people have been cleaner than ever. In Islam, it is part of our faith that we are clean. Allah says,

"Surely Allah loves those who always turn to Him in repentance and those who purify themselves." [Al-Quran, 2:222]

Being clean benefits us to also stay healthy. Those who are not clean will not enter Jannah. Now, everybody tries their hardest to be clean. So, it helps them, those around them, and their path in Islam.

Online school is good for us because we need education. We still can learn in quarantine by having online school on screen, not in person. We can use online resources to learn more about Islamic laws. People use this time to learn more information. Many people don't have the materials for online learning so those who do should be grateful. The first ayah revealed in the Quran tells us to learn by reading,

"Read, (O Prophet) in the Name of your Lord Who created—" [Al-Quran; 96:1]

Family time is supposed to be precious and important. Before, we were not able to spend much time with our families because we had school or work. But now, we stay with our families at home. You can go on walks, eat lunch, and pray together. Spending time with your family also helps with learning more new things.

In conclusion, cleanliness, online learning, and family time are blessings from Allah during Covid-19. Being clean benefits everybody. Family time makes your life more fun and happier. Online education helps us learn even in our home. We should be so grateful for all these blessings from Allah and always remember him.

Young Muslim Voices

Special Recognition – Speech: Raniya Miller
Al-Rahmah School, Baltimore, MD

Muslims have faced many challenges due to the pandemic of the Coronavirus, such as losing family, not going to masjid, and not being able to see their family members. But there are some blessings because of this, too. It is hard to notice them sometimes because we may feel like Covid-19 has ruined our lives. But if you stop and think, then you will see there are some blessings because of this. These are some of the blessings that my family had during the Coronavirus pandemic.

The first blessing my family had been spending more time with the people with us right now, including my mom, dad, brother, grandparents, and aunt. We used to just spend time with our friends, but now we spend more time with the people who are living with us and near us. Now we know more about each other and have bonded more.

The second blessing my family had was clean air. Air is a very important thing for everyone. We all need air to live. Because there is Coronavirus, people do not go in their cars that much anymore. Cars can cause air pollution. Air pollution is bad because you can breathe in toxins that can make you sick, it's bad for the environment, and it can damage crops, plants, and trees. That is why air pollution is bad and why clean air is a blessing.

The last blessing, I would like to share, that my family had was having less school! This is my favorite blessing because instead of 7 hours of school a day, we have about 4! This may not seem much of a blessing, but it is to me. This is a good blessing because I have less stress over work, breaks between classes, and I can watch tv during breaks. And I get to choose the shows! That is why this is my favorite blessing.

So, these are some blessings my family had during Covid-19. Even though things were hard during Covid-19, and we faced a lot of challenges, we still did not forget to be grateful. I hope you stay grateful too!

MIDDLE SCHOOL | LEVEL 3

Topic:

The entire world has been struggling with the disruption of the coronavirus, however, for Muslims, our way of life is such that we have ways of coping with this pandemic. In light of the Quran and Sunnah, describe how Muslims have been using their faith to positively impact their communities even when they are facing hardships.

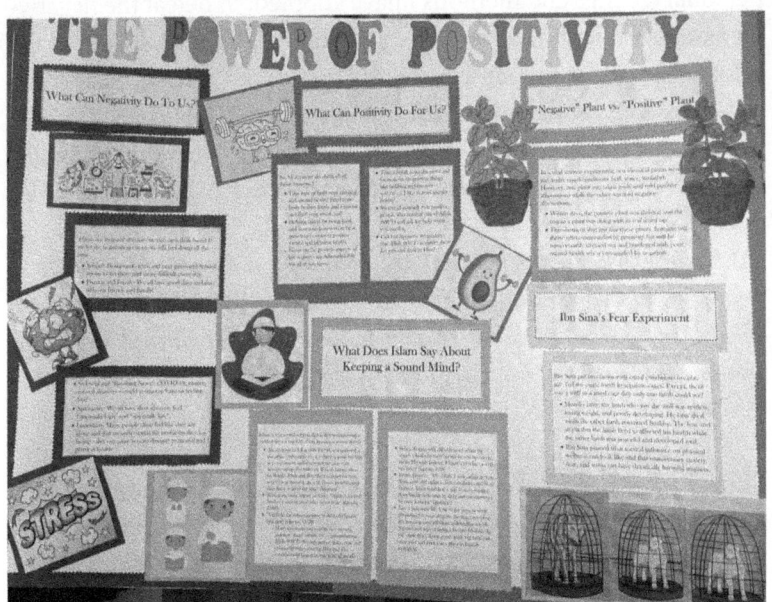

This poster was submitted by Musa Rahmani of level 3.

1st Place: Yusuf Mehmood
MCC, Silver Spring, MD

Chirp, chirp, chirp. The night is dark, the stars are out, do you hear the crickets at my anti-COVID19 campsite? I am getting ready for the great pandemic storm! I have three tents available today for you to see. The three tents are my personal experiences tent, the family tent, and the community tent. Let me take you through each tent and show you how they have helped me get through this pandemic. Each tent is special in its own way, but together they have the power to overcome the negativity from the COVID19 windstorm.

The first tent is the personal experiences tent. This tent displays my personal feelings and methods I have adopted, to defeat the negativity associated with the pandemic. During COVID 19, I have made a lot of personal dua and increased my dhikr. I have been more self-conscious with Allah and the Prophet Muhamad's (SAWS) teachings. I have memorized some duas that are heavy on the scale. Abu Hurairah (RA) reported: The Messenger of Allah (SAWS) said,

"There are two statements that are light for the tongue to remember, heavy in the scales and are dear to the Merciful: "Subhan-Allahi wa bihamdihi, Subhan-Allahil-Azeem [Glory be to Allah and His is the praise, (and) Allah, the Greatest is free from imperfection)." [Sahih Al-Bukhari]

Since I have been home more, I have been able to memorize new surahs and read more Quran. The COVID crisis has affected my life, but I try my best to stay calm and think about Allah and the Prophet (SAWS). This tent is full of gratitude and new personal growth for me.

Moving on to the second tent, we have my family's experiences. We have been spending a lot of family quality time together. My parents cut fruit for us every night, tell us stories, we play board games, carry out food and eat in the van together- picnic style. I am grateful that my family is safe from the virus. My father is a frontline doctor and received his vaccine, Alhamdullilah. My family has also started listening to lectures about the Prophet (SAWS) and we recite adhkar together. During the crisis my grandpa had gotten sepsis and had to go to the hospital, my family and I made so much dua for him. We were all scared for him at that moment, but Allah answered our duas and he got better. This second tent displays my family's experiences during this pandemic. We learned to spend more time together and huddle closer to each other in this tent. Our connection to Allah allowed us to better our connection to each other.

The last tent is the community tent. In the community, my sister and I have been volunteering to do work on a horse farm. I have helped to feed, groom, and check the horses for cuts and scrapes. I have also been taking out the trash and aim to have a cleaner community. I pray I receive good deeds for helping the community. I have been aiming to help the community just like the Prophet (SAWS). My family has been donating to Islamic institutions. I know that my community needs support, so I try my best to help out. This third tent has shown me creative ways I can help my community during this unconventional time.

In conclusion, I believe that 2020 has been hard for us, but we have made it through this year of hardship and loss. I have hiked my way through these pandemic trails, but I know Allah says in the Quran:

"We will certainly test you with a touch of fear and famine and loss of property, life, and crops. Give good news to those who patiently endure— who, when faced with a disaster, say, "Surely to Allah we belong and to Him we will (all) return." They are the ones who will receive Allah's blessings and mercy. And it is they who are (rightly) guided." [Al-Quran; 2: 155-157]

Young Muslim Voices

When I leave all my affairs to Allah, I am at peace. The tents of my personal experience, my family, and my community are pegged in deeply and firmly. The winds of the pandemic cannot blow down these three strong tents!

2nd Place: Mariyah Mehmood
MCC, Silver Spring, MD

Sparkle, shiny and glamorous! Have you seen anything like it? The dazzling crown from the COVID 19 dynasty has arrived! It is said that the person who can wear this crown will be able to overcome the COVID crisis. There are three unique and stunning jewels placed strategically on the crown. Further analysis of the gems shows us the positive lessons you can learn during COVID 19. The first jaw-dropping green jewel represents my personal experience. The next stunning red jewel represents my family's experience during this difficult time. The last majestic blue jewel represents my community. Let us explore this powerful crown and its three gems in detail.

The first jaw-dropping green gem in this glorious crown represents my personal experience during the pandemic. I am relying on Allah to help me weave my way out. During the pandemic, I experienced a lot of hardships such as fear, loneliness, sadness and anxiety. Since I was not going to school anymore, I had more time to focus on my spirituality. I swapped out the negative emotions I was feeling with positivity like prayer, Quran, dhikr and duas. During the pandemic, I have been memorizing Surah Mulk. I find myself reciting and learning new adhkaar (supplications) during the quiet moments. Allah says in the Quran:

"So, surely with hardship comes ease. Surely with (that) hardship comes (more) ease." [Al-Quran; 94:5-6]

I have begun spending some time after each prayer sitting quietly and making dua. With this exercise I feel like all my worries and stresses disappear, I put them in Allah's Hands. Journaling my feelings has been an essential tool. These are the wonderful blessings that make the green gem burn bright in my crown during COVID 19.

The second stunning red jewel represents my family. My family has been a great resource to help me stay positive and remember Allah (SWT). We learned that reciting Durood helps when I feel anxious. Practicing gratitude as a family has been a fun exercise. My father is a physician, fighting COVID 19 on the frontlines. I am grateful that my father was able to receive the vaccine. I learned that

"Allah does not require of any soul more than what it can afford..."
[Al-Quran; 2:286]

Hardships are given to make us come closer to Allah. During the pandemic, my grandfather became ill with sepsis and had to go to the hospital. This was a fearful time for my family, as he was there alone. We made copious amounts of dua and alhamdullilah, and after two weeks he came home. This radiant red jewel in my crown shows the power of family overcoming the negativity of COVID 19 together.

The last magnificent blue jewel represents my community. Serving the community during a time of social distancing has been challenging. But I love a good challenge! My brother and I go to a horse farm once a week to volunteer. We help feed the horses, groom them, clean their stalls, and check if they are healthy and don't have any cuts or scrapes. My father told me that the Sahabas (companions of the Prophet (SAWS)) would also tend horses and ride them. If you have the intention to be like the Sahaba, the best of people, and complete these tasks for the sake of Allah you can also get rewarded and have fun at the same time. During this pandemic, many families have lost their jobs and do not have food or money. I raise funds and donate to the zakat foundation in my local masjid. The community is resilient and will carve their way through the canyon of hardships. The blue jewel shines bright with hope and as a community we will overcome this pandemic.

In conclusion, I am confident we will make it through COVID 19 and come out a Queen insha'Allah. My crown with the three radiant gems of my personal experience, my family and my community will illuminate the way through. We will continue to rely on Allah, stay positive, keep motivating each other, pray, make dhikr and increase our dua. With this jeweled crown on my head, I see a bright path ahead. The darkness of COVID 19 is trying to envelop the kingdom, it will never affect us if we work together, are grateful and stay positive!

Young Muslim Voices

3rd Place: Sumayyah Islam
Diyanet Center of America, Lanham, MD

Assalamu Alaikum Warahmatullahi Wabarakatuh

In the Quran, Allah says,

"Indeed, in the Messenger of Allah you have an excellent example for whoever has hope in Allah and the Last Day and remembers Allah often." [Al-Quran 33:21]

Even almost 1400 years after the Prophet's death, we still emulate his way of life and try to implement it into our own lives, in order to become better Muslims. His teachings, words, and adab are not only an example to the Ummah, but they have also influenced many people beyond just Muslims. This pandemic has been a struggle for many families across my community. Alhamdulillah, I am blessed with enough food and shelter for our family to be sufficient, but not everyone has the same situation. As Muslims, it is our duty to help our neighbors and Muslim brothers and sisters in times of need. Although I may be young, it is still possible to make a positive impact on the community around me.

The easiest way for us to make change in our communities is to start with what is close to us, our families. In the Quran, Allah says,

"O humanity! Be mindful of your Lord Who created you from a single soul, and from it He created its mate, and through both He spread countless men and women. And be mindful of Allah—in Whose Name you appeal to one another—and (honor) family ties. Surely Allah is ever Watchful over you." [Al-Quran; 4:1]

Allah tells us to "honor" our family relationships, which includes that we take care of them. Alhamdulillah, my parents and siblings have been healthy throughout the pandemic. However, my grandparents who live away from us have some health issues, and it can be very dangerous for them to go outside since they are older. Because of this, it is difficult for them to get groceries. Taking Allah's words into account, I help my family get groceries for my grandparents and deliver them to their house to make it easy for them.

Because of the COVID-19 pandemic, Muslim families around our community have lost their jobs and with that, have a hard time getting enough food for their families. The Prophet warns Muslims in a hadith,

"He is not a believer whose stomach is filled while his neighbor goes hungry." [Al-Adab Al-Mufrad]

All around us there are families that go hungry because of the pandemic. I sometimes go with my father in order to deliver food boxes to families that are struggling with food.

Another way is to help our direct neighbors, even if they are not Muslim. The Prophet (SAWS) prescribes that we help our neighbor when they ask for help. My next-door neighbor does not speak English that well, and sometimes has a hard time with their homework. I try to help them with their homework as best as I can.

During the day, I recite the Quran because my goal in life is to become a hafiza. Whenever my parents test me on my recitation, I remind them that every day we should recite the Quran to get a numerous amount of good deeds and have more knowledge about Islam. During the weekend, my family sits down in the living room, and we put on a lecture on the TV about something we should all work on or something that we should know. After salah, we frequently talk about the Quran or read some hadiths about salah or something useful in our Islamic life.

During the first revolution in the Prophet Muhammad's time, Abu Lahab and his followers gave Prophet Muhammad (SAWS) a hard time to spread the word about Islam. The Prophet usually got harassed and insulted, but the Prophet stayed calm and was still on his feet. Today, people feel they have hard times like the Prophet, but they usually go astray or violent. They put the blame on others on why they are that way. They start listening to shaytan and do things that always bring them a step away from Allah.

If we have hard times, we should stay patient and have trust and faith in Allah so that He can guide us to the straight path and help us go through these difficult times. Ever since the global pandemic, it has split all of our family members, friends, and community away from us. It has been hard to be split from the people you love but Allah's faith has given us some hope in this terrible time.

Special Recognition – Essay: Saad Mahfuz
Diyanet Center of America, Lanham, MD

In March 2020 the world locked down because of the deadly Coronavirus which would become a pandemic that would kill a million people. Businesses shut down, sporting events were postponed, in-person classes were canceled, and hospitals were unable to keep up with the amount of patients admitted every day. To stop the spread of the Coronavirus, health experts advised people to stay home and only leave for essential items. To follow these rules, my family and I stayed home. Personally, watching this entire situation happen, I began to grow sad since I was unable to see my Imam at the Masjid, play with my closest friends and relatives outside, and watch my favorite sports on T.V. At the time, I thought this sudden switch in my life would be difficult to get used to. However, as time went on, I realized the many blessings Allah (SWT) had given us that were not obvious at first.

The blessings my family and I enjoyed, because of the lockdown, came in many forms. To begin with, no one had anywhere to go, so we all had more free time. As a result, we were able to take advantage of our foosball table, basketball arcade, and bean bag toss and play against each other as a family. Some nights, we gathered to watch a movie! The fun my family and I had, made us all grateful for the blessing of having free time. Before the Coronavirus, this was hard to get since everyone always had somewhere to be and something to do.

Besides family fun time, my family and I had the huge blessing of worshiping Allah (SWT) together. We listened to lectures but most importantly, we were able to pray more of the five daily prayers together and Tahajjud sometimes. When Ramadan and Eid came along, we celebrated together. During Ramadan, we prepared Iftars, ate as a family, and prayed Taraweeh salah which was led by my two elder brothers. On Eid, we prepared special food, dressed up, and remembered Allah (SWT). Spending every day and night in the worship of Allah (SWT) together was a great blessing.

Normally, my family members would be busy at work or school, but the Coronavirus situation had forced us to pause our busyness and earn good deeds together.

In the beginning of the Coronavirus, I was nervous about how to keep myself entertained. I wanted to have fun but stay safe at the same time. Despite my thoughts that came along with adjusting to this new life, my family and I were still able to create a fun time together through different activities and the worship of Allah (SWT). Today, the Coronavirus vaccine has been released and in sha Allah the end of this pandemic is near, and the world will return back to normal. Alhamdullilah, I am really grateful for all the blessings that Allah (SWT) has given me and my family during this lockdown and hope to continue doing all our activities and good deeds together, inshaAllah.

Special Recognition – Speech: Adam Khan
ADAMS Center, VA

The COVID-19 virus has caused many families around the world to struggle both physically and mentally. Muslims are using their faith and teachings to help the elders as well as our parents to donate to the community and to social distance from the elders and everyone alike to avoid spreading the virus. Using our beliefs, Muslims have been able to help our community with their needs using the Prophet's teachings.

Muslims know that respecting and helping the elders greatly improves the well-being of everyone in the community. Each week, the elderly is brought food and water, their rent is paid for by the Mosque and they are called every few days to make sure they feel like they are being supported. During COVID-19, members have learned to stay six feet away from each other in order to keep everybody safe. The Prophet also helped his wives by cooking and cleaning around the house. Muslims have used this teaching of helping others through actions that may be unusual. This is reflected by calling people we usually wouldn't do and checking on their wellbeing. He also had good qualities such as caring for orphans and single mothers. Helping and respecting parents is important because parents have given up so much for their children. So, by helping around the house, parents can see that their sacrifice is appreciated.

The Prophet tells us that everyone in the community is considered a family. If anyone mourns the loss of a loved one, then all community members mourn. If no one donated hard work and time to help others, then there would be no community. This idea abandons everyone in their suffering; therefore, Muslims are taught to help.

Praying for others is helpful, especially for those who are quarantined, like the elderly or small children. We pray for the well beings of ourselves and others five times a day. If you are praying for someone or yourself, you are supposed to pray for yourself first then for other people. For example, if you don't help yourself, you can't help other people if you are the one who needs help first. We also practice patience because this is a difficult time where all our loved ones are suffering and it's also a teaching of the prophet. There is a saying that God has mentioned,

"So, surely with hardship comes ease." [Al-Quran; 94:5]

Using this teaching, we are able to overcome our sadness. Using our beliefs to help those around us during the pandemic has taught me that anything can happen at any time if God wills, and to use our time wisely. We should use what we have wisely even if it's a little bit and take care of our community, but most importantly, our beloved ones. Looking at the pandemic with a positive mindset allows us to see the benefits of the pandemic that others may not see. Always remember there's a light at the end of the tunnel!

MIDDLE SCHOOL | LEVEL 4

Topic:

The entire world has been struggling with the disruption of the coronavirus, however, for Muslims, our way of life is such that we have ways of coping with this pandemic. In light of the Quran and Sunnah, describe how Muslims have been using their faith to positively impact their communities even when they are facing hardships.

Young Muslim Voices

1st Place: Laiba M. Monir
Dumbarton Middle School, Baltimore, MD

COVID-19, also known as coronavirus, a pandemic that still claws and bites at our dunya and its inhabitants today, started in November 2019, and hasn't ended yet. Due to the virus, everyone has had to go into lockdown, a dull period of staying at home with online school, minimal socialization, and rare moments of leaving the house. During this time, I have been using my faith and teachings of the Prophet Muhammad (SAWS) to impact my family and community by fulfilling my social responsibilities, staying grateful, giving charity, keeping contact with relatives, and praying in congregation with my family.

I have been fulfilling my social responsibilities placed upon me by the Prophet (SAWS) during quarantine. The Prophet (SAWS) mentioned four social responsibilities of the believers, which are: to make things easy, not to make things difficult, to make people happy, and not to repel them. I have been making things easy for others by helping around the house and alleviating stress for my parents, both of whom have work. I have not been making things difficult for others by staying inside to avoid the spread of germs. I have been making people happy by virtually communicating with my friends and spending a lot of time with my family so that no one gets bored or unmotivated in quarantine. I have not been repelling anyone but instead becoming closer to those around me. In these ways, I am fulfilling my social responsibilities placed upon me by the Prophet's (SAWS) teachings during quarantine.

I have been grateful during the lockdown. The Prophet (SAWS) named three things as the best property, one of which was *"a grateful heart"* *[Sunan At-Tirmidhi]*. Alhamdulillah, many events have blessed me in quarantine, such as more attention coming to the Black Lives Matter movement and the mistreatment of Uighur Muslims, staying safe from the virus, being able to do everything from home, and the development of a vaccine against COVID-19. I thank Allah (SWT) for His blessings regularly and keep in mind that I am very blessed during this situation and that many have it much worse than me. For this reason, I have been following another teaching of the Prophet (SAWS): Sadaqah (charity).

I have been committing to Sadaqah and participating in giving charity to the unfortunate during the pandemic. In a hadith narrated by Al-Bukhari, the Prophet (SAWS) said:

"Protect yourself from hell-fire even by giving a piece of date as charity." [Sahih Al-Bukhari]

My family and I cook large trays of food every Sunday and deliver them to refugees and generally unfortunate people. In Islam, it is crucial to give charity if one can, as everyone is equal in Allah's (SWT) eyes regardless of economic status and should help each other out in times of need.

During the lockdown, I have been keeping constant contact with my relatives, whether close or distant. Prophet (SAWS) said:

"He who believes in Allah and the Last Day, let him maintain good relation with kin…" [Sahih Al-Bukhari]

Unfortunately, I cannot meet with them and communicate in person, so I regularly call, message, and make dua for them. Even though they are far from me in body, Allah (SWT) has kept them with me in soul, prayer, and dua.

Finally, during quarantine, I have been praying every prayer in congregation with my family on time.

"And enjoin prayer upon your family [and people] and be steadfast therein," [Al-Quran; 20:132]

My family and I have become much closer with Allah (SWT) during the pandemic, preferring praying together, as in Islam, praying in congregation is much more beneficial for each member. We consider Fajr, Dhuhur, Asr, Maghrib, and Isha as a time for mindfulness, spirituality, peace, connection with Allah (SWT), and silent connection with other family members.

In summary, I have been using my faith and teachings of the Prophet Muhammad (SAWS) to impact my family and community by fulfilling my social responsibilities, staying grateful, giving charity, keeping contact with relatives, and praying in a family congregation.

2nd Place: Dawud Qaadri
Home School, Lanham, MD

The coronavirus has impacted many lives across the globe. The way that my community and my family have dealt with this pandemic has been by using the Qur'an and Sunnah to make living in these times easier. Feeding the community, having trust in Allah and helping however you can. There are three ways to do this.

Because of this pandemic, many people are without jobs, food, and money. One of the local masjids in my community, The Islamic Community Center of Laurel, has held food distributions for the local community. The reason why the community did this was so that they can help the people who are being impacted by Covid-19 in the community. We know from the hadith that Prophet Muhammad (SAWS) said:

"He is not a believer whose stomach is filled while the neighbor to his side is hungry." [Al-Adab Al-Mufrad]

Knowing this, ICCL took action and has had food distributions ever since the pandemic came to Maryland.

In the Quran, Allah says:

"Indeed, with hardships [will be] ease." [Al-Quran; 94:6]

So, after this hardship (Covid-19) there will be ease InshaAllah. Knowing this, we should have trust in Allah that He will help us when we need help. When COVID-19 started, there was fear and nervousness (hardship). But now, we are not as scared because vaccines are coming out and now, we have more knowledge about the virus, so this brought us some ease. InshaAllah we will all experience the ease of Covid-19 going away.

We, as Muslims, should always help those who need help. For example: if your neighbor cannot go to work because of this pandemic, they are likely struggling.

This is where we need to step in and give them assistance because this is what Islam teaches us. If we are people that cannot make money, then we should have patience and pray to Allah. Because Allah says in the Quran:

"O you who have believed, seek help through patience and prayer. Indeed, Allah is with the patient." [Al-Quran; 2:153]

And one of the greatest honors in this world is for Allah to be on your side. If Allah is on your side, then He will protect you. Or if you continue to get tested then know that it is part of Allah's ultimate plan.

In conclusion, doing these three things is a good way to help get your community through the pandemic. By feeding your community, trusting Allah to help you, and helping your neighbors you can use your faith to help get through the pandemic. I wish everyone well in this pandemic and InshaAllah we can all find goodness out of this hardship.

3rd Place: Tasneem Syeda- Ali
Home School, Gaithersburg, MD

Coping with the COVID-19 pandemic has been a very challenging test. However, I am exceedingly grateful for my faith. Using the Qur'an and Sunnah as a guide to live through this hardship is very essential. By obeying the Qur'an and Sunnah we can pass through this test. Allah says in the Qur'an:

"Say, "Obey Allah and the Messenger..."" [Al-Quran; 3:32]

Everyone has different tests that Allah gives them, but many are able to turn it into something positive. Even when facing difficulties in life, it is still possible for many to bring a positive influence on others. Nothing, other than Allah's will, can stop us from bringing good and happiness to our communities. Making a positive impact starts in our own home. Aisha (RA) reported that RasulAllah (SAWS) said,

"The best of you is he who is best to his family..." [Sunan At-Tirmidhi]

We are all stuck in our homes; this is the best time to strengthen our relationships with our families. Everyone plays an important role in their families. It does not matter how small an impact we make; it still matters, and we still matter! One of my favorite impacts I had on my family was praying in Jama'at. With the closure of our Masjid, we were extremely sad, so I knew I had to make a difference. Alhamdulillah, I put together a schedule and we started to pray together. I pray this impact will forever stay in my family. Ibn Umar (RA) narrates that RasulAllah (SAWS) said:

"Salat in congregation is twenty-seven times more meritorious than a Salat performed individually." [Sahih Al- Bukhari]

Taking it one step further, our community- regardless of our age, we matter in our communities. A critical way to bring a positive impact in our community is to help. Helping is a way to relieve our own hardship. Whether it is helping in local food drives or helping our neighbors, it is all considered as helping. AbuHurairah (RA) narrates, RasulAllah (SAWS) said:

"Whoever relieves a Muslim of a burden from the burdens of the world, Allah will relieve him of a burden from the burdens on the Day of Judgement. And whoever helps ease a difficulty in the world, Allah will grant him ease from a difficulty in the world and in the Hereafter." [Sunan At-Tirmidhi]

Furthermore, it is significant to know that even without uttering a word we can bring positive effects. Simply by wearing a mask we can change the mindset of another person- by seeing us that person might put on their mask too.

Stuck at home? Looking for what to do? Send Dawah letters. For me, specifically, I sent letters to my favorite quarterbacks, including my favorite quarterback, Josh Allen. Insha'Allah someday someone will respond. Even though I think that, most probably, I will not get a response; only Allah knows! The reward for giving Dawah, and Allah guiding someone through me, is so huge, I would be foolish to let this great opportunity down. Sahl Ibn Sa'd (RA) reported: Rasulullah (SAWS) said,

"By Allah, if one man is guided on the right path (i.e., converted to Islam) through you, it would be better for you than (a great number of) red camels" [Sahih Al-Bukhari 2847]

In conclusion, these were some of the positive influences I had on my family and community. It is important to use the Qur'an and Sunnah as a reminder. Many people before us had faced trials far greater than the ones we face today. My dear Muslims, remember the story of the Hijra, if the Quraysh looked to their feet, they would have spotted Rasulullah (SAWS) and Abu Bakr (RA). Rasulullah (SAWS) calmly said as found in the Qur'an:

"...and he [i.e., Muḥammad] said to his companion, "Do not grieve; indeed, Allah is with us." [Al-Quran; 9:40]

Recall, in the story of Musa (AS), when the army of the Fir'awn, was behind them and there was water in front of them, what was the response of Musa (AS) to his people when the people said, as found in the Qur'an:

"And when the two companies saw one another, the companions of Moses said, "Indeed, we are to be overtaken!" [Moses] said, "No! Indeed, with me is my Lord; He will guide me.""" [Al-Quran; 26:61-62]

Ponder, how Allah has shown us the light after four years, as we rejoiced on November 7, 2020. Indeed, on that day Allah saved our democracy. Muslims participated and Alhamdulillah, Muslim votes matter! Contemplate, after how many years did Allah give the Buffalo Bills an AFC East title? Twenty-five years! Yet, they still did not lose hope. How then can us Muslims lose hope? My dear Muslims I leave you with one question to ponder upon: do we want to lose hope, when indeed the help of Allah is near?

Young Muslim Voices

Special Recognition – Essay: Ruwad Islam
Al-Huda School, College Park, MD

Did you know that over 1.5 million people died due to coronavirus? Nearly every country is struggling to reduce the spread of this dreadful virus. It's difficult to stay positive during such a trying time. Not only are people dying from this virus, but many are also losing their homes due to financial troubles and others are unable to see their loved ones as they follow social distancing rules. However, as Muslims, we must have faith in Allah and do our best to give back to our communities and find ways to cope with Covid-19. The Quran and the teachings of the Prophet Muhammad (SAWS) are the perfect sources to use in positively impacting our families and local communities during this pandemic. In the Quran, in Surah Al- Qasas, Allah says:

"Those will be given their reward twice for what they patiently endured and [because] they avert evil through good, and from what We have provided them they spend." [Al-Quran; 28:54]

This ayah is talking about how important it is to stay patient when things don't go as planned. Covid- 19 was definitely unexpected, and many of us have been stuck at home with our families. Before Covid, everyone was at school or work, so it was easy to have our own time before being with each other. However, with everyone at home, it can start to feel crowded, and people can get easily upset with each other. Personally, I had moments when I would get upset with my younger sister because I just wanted to play games, but she wanted to do something with me. People might not want to help around the house and only stay in their rooms. However, this ayah teaches us the beauty of patience and its great reward. Even though people might not want to be stuck at home every day, it is important to stay patient with one another. Consequently, we learn that being patient will not just reward us but also have a positive impact on our families.

Although many have been stuck at home with families, there are many resources available to connect with schools and community organizations virtually. For example, even though students cannot go back to school in person, there are many ways to positively impact places outside of one's home. The Prophet Muhammad (SAWS) said:

"Charity does not decrease wealth, no one forgives another except that Allah increases his honor, and no one humbles himself for the sake of Allah except that Allah raises his status." [Sahih Muslim]

Charity elevates one's status. This year, with Covid-19, many people have lost hope because they may have lost their jobs or homes and times are tough. It is important to give for the sake of Allah because it not only helps those in need but also gives you a higher status in front of Allah. Every year, my school has a donation competition to raise money for the school and sell tickets for a fundraising dinner. However, due to Covid-19, the 2020 competition was different. There was no fundraising dinner, so students had to raise money for the school virtually. Nonetheless, many people still donated to the school even though they would not be attending an extravagant dinner. Raising money and partaking in this competition had a positive impact on my school. It showed that even during such tough times people are willing to give back to their local school and community. By giving, they are elevating their statuses in front of Allah.

With all these virtual tools available, it still is not the same as doing activities in person, causing impatience and displeasure. Kids, for example, would rather go see their friends at school or hang out with people outside of their homes. However, strict rules have been set by the states to stay indoors and remain in quarantine. Above all, the Prophet (SAWS) said,

"When you hear of it (a plague) in a land do not go to it, and if it occurs in a land while you are in it do not go out fleeing from it." [Sahih Al-Bukhari]

This hadith talks about quarantine, which is exactly what we have been asked to do this past year. The Prophet is advising his followers about how to handle a plague and the importance of quarantining ourselves. He also said,

"Do not put a patient with a healthy person." [Sahih Al-Bukhari]

He extended the teachings to animals and told his followers that the cattle suffering from diseases should not be mixed with healthy cattle. This hadith talks about social distancing. The Prophet is saying that a sick person should not be near a healthy person. Social distancing and quarantine both positively impact our communities, and the country overall, because it helps contain the virus and slow down its spread.

With so many people contracting the coronavirus, and many even dying from it, it's no wonder as to why we must follow social distancing rules and resort to online tools. However, it can become difficult for us to do something we are not used to and going back to our old habits can be tempting. Nonetheless, we should refer to the Quran and Sunnah to help us create a positive impact around us. At home, we can stay patient with our families. At school, we can raise money virtually. And finally, we can continue to social distance and quarantine ourselves as a means of protection. These are just some of the many ways to positively impact our homes, schools, and local communities during this negative time.

Special Recognition – Speech: Saadiq Ahmed
Home School, Beltsville, MD

It is very important for Muslims to have a point of reference when we face any kind of hardships in life. The Quran and the teachings of the Prophet (SAWS) are the two sources that if we follow them, any kind of challenge in life becomes easy. In the beginning of this pandemic, the news was: "coronavirus is spreading". So, people went crazy, and they all piled into the stores to get all the food and cleaning supplies they can get. However, did Allah create this world-wide crisis for us to just be greedy and go crazy? The year 2020 was a very difficult year for everyone. A lot of people lost family and friends because of the coronavirus infection. So many businesses that relied on large amounts of people coming and going lost their jobs. Hundreds of thousands of kids all over the world had to adjust to "home-schooling". Everybody had to learn to do things differently. And yet–no one could have imagined any of this just a few months before. For so many people, life had become difficult, unbearable, frustrating, and completely unpredictable. Why was it so difficult, however? Especially for Muslims who should remember what Allah says in the Quran,

"Do they not see that they are tried every year once or twice but then they do not repent, nor do they remember?" [Al-Quran; 9:126]

It is because Allah was testing us and through it, we should have been praying more, reading more Quran, asking Allah to forgive us for our sins and relying more on Allah. However, a lot of people just sat around and did nothing. They were too afraid to go out or do anything with their lives. Their fear overcame them as they forgot that Allah is the one who could take away all of their fears. That is not how we are supposed to live our lives during a test from Allah.

During the pandemic, my parents did not feel it would be safe for us to do the things we would normally do like go to the store with them or even get together with our friends. Being at home 24 hours a day, 7 days a week was not something I had ever imagined I would have to do. When the weather was good, we did play outside and go hiking but it was not often enough. Shortly after the pandemic was underway, Ramadan was here. Usually, this is a time of great anticipation for me. Ramadan usually has a different feel than in the rest of the months. I like to see which masjid we were going to go for iftaar and for Taraweeh prayers and which of my friends I would get to see. However, this would not be the case because of the pandemic. So, I decided that I would make the most out of the situation. First, I made sure to keep reading my Quran as much as possible and pray on time since we had nowhere to go. Also, I began to help my parents prepare for iftaar and Taraweeh prayers at home. We took advantage of the family time and listened to many lectures that were now online. Ramadan ended up being very special last year and one that I will never forget, alhamdulillah. Staying positive throughout the first few months really helped us be patient during Ramadan when it is usually a time when the brothers and sisters of a community bond more.

Thankfully, because we are in a community, many other opportunities came up that made me feel like I could actually make myself useful and positively impact my community and my family. There were several food drives in our area. My parents volunteered me and my siblings to help fill up grocery bags with different items that would be given out to those in need and to community members. I also helped unload and distribute several gallons of milk to the community. Standing in those cold trucks was exciting and an experience I will never forget. Alhamdulillah for these opportunities.

In conclusion, Muslims are not supposed to become too fearful of the challenges and tests Allah brings our way. During this coronavirus pandemic, we learned that we have to do our part by washing our hands and wearing masks whenever we were out. However, we also have to make ourselves useful and use the blessings from Allah to help others. My strategy for maintaining a positive attitude and having a good impact on my family and community was to be patient, keep making dua and turning back to Allah each time I felt like the world was going to be over soon. When my Mom's Uncle died because of COVID, it hit me very hard. This made me realize what I had learned about what the Prophet (SAWS) said about how Allah tests us. The Prophet (SAWS) said,

"The servant shall continue to be tried until he is left walking upon the earth without any sins." (Sunan At- Tirmidhi)

For the believer, being patient in times of hardship is a means to be purified, in sha Allah. I make so much dua that my Mom's Uncle was purified before he died in sha Allah. I will keep making dua that this pandemic is over soon, and we can get back to seeing our friends and family again on a daily basis, Insha Allah.

HIGH SCHOOL | LEVEL 5

Topic:

Some say the coronavirus pandemic is a punishment, some say it is a test. Either way, what should the mindset of a Muslim be during a global event of this scale and how should that translate into productive action?

Young Muslim Voices

1st Place: Nabeel Chowdhury
Al-Huda School, College Park, MD

COVID-19. The virus that made 2020 infamously known as one of the worst years in the history of mankind. Some say it is a punishment. Some say it is a test. I believe it is what the individual interprets it to be. Personally, I believe it is a test. Regardless, as Muslims, we must always have faith that every situation has a bright side because Allah has put us in that situation. We must try to make the best out of any circumstance. Never hold your head down and keep working to be a productive member of society. In the case of this COVID-19 pandemic, Allah put the entire world in this test, regardless of age, race, or gender. We should be helping people in any way we can, without putting ourselves or the people close to us in danger. Along with that, now is the best time to be praying to Allah for the wellbeing of our family and friends, and for helping us throughout these hard times. As Muslims, even during a global pandemic of this scale, we must have a mindset that translates into productive action. As now most of us have an abundance of time, we should use our free time wisely, follow the protocols to not endanger ourselves or anyone else, and be patient during these unprecedented times.

Due to this pandemic, most of us have gained an abundance of free time. School, work, and extracurriculars have all gone virtual, making days feel shorter and more stress-free. This has allowed us more time to do things that we previously would not have been able to do due to shortage of time. However, not all of us realize the blessing Allah has given us through our abundance of free time. In a Hadith narrated by Bukhari, our beloved Prophet Muhammad (SAWS) said:

"There are two blessings in which many people incur loss. (They are) health and free time (for doing good)." [Sahih Al-Bukhari]

So, we must be grateful for all the free time Allah has given us to keep actively obtaining His blessings. However, even with all this free time, we must be careful with how we use it. In a Hadith narrated by Ibn Abbas, the Prophet (SAWS) said:

"Take advantage of five before five: your youth before your old age, your health before your illness, your riches before your poverty, your free time before your work, and your life before your death." [Shu'ab al-Iman]

We can take advantage of three out of the five things mentioned in this Hadith. We never know when we might contract this virus, so we must do what we can while we are healthy or before we die. We should also use our free time wisely before we no longer have any more of it. But how do we spend all that free time?

Try doing new things. In a time that everything has gone virtual, online learning is now more accessible than ever before, and not just with school. There are extra classes that you can take, even if they are offered overseas. This gives a wide variety of new things for us to try out from the comfort of our own home. The thing is, all these platforms such as YouTube or Zoom are not new, but we have been put in a situation where using them has become more prominent in our time. Previously, it was harder to find time to do productive things outside of school and work, such as listen to lectures by Imams. There are so many that have been posted on YouTube, and now, we finally have time to spare to expand our knowledge. However, filling up all your extra time with activities online can start to become overwhelming. Therefore, it is important to make a schedule to help stay organized. Organization is key to a productive lifestyle.

With all these new extracurriculars that you start investing your free time in, it can get easily repetitive. Even though it is more convenient for things to be virtual, some people prefer things to be done in person. Additionally, people may want to start seeing their friends and family. However, we must follow all the strict guidelines such as wearing masks and staying six feet apart to slow down the spread of the coronavirus. Even the Prophet (SAWS) has advised us in the case of these situations. Sau'd reported: The Prophet (SAWS) said,

"If you hear of an outbreak of plague in a land, do not enter it; but if the plague breaks out in a place while you are in it, do not leave that place." [Sahih Al-Bukhari]

This hadith is especially relevant during this pandemic. We know that the coronavirus is a highly contagious virus, so we must try to limit our outings, especially to places that put us at risk. At the same time, if we are in an area that makes us prone to the virus, then we must not go to other places to prevent spreading the virus. This ensures our safety as well the safety of our friends and family. Though we may want to meet them in person, we must follow these guidelines, not only because they are what our states have ordered, but also because they have been advised by our Prophet Muhammad (SAWS). It is difficult to do something we are not accustomed to, but we must stay patient.

There are three types of patience, all of which are applicable in our current situation. The first type of patience is patience in doing good deeds. Due to the pandemic, we have more free time to do good deeds. For example, we can take an hour or two out of our day to read the Quran. We could pray all the Sunnah prayers along with all the mandatory ones. There are many more good deeds that can be done, and it would be difficult to list them all. The second type of patience is patience in refraining from bad deeds. More free time means more boredom, which can tempt people into doing things that they should not be doing. We must be patient and tolerate the urge to do something bad. The third type of patience is patience during times of crisis and hardship. Muslims should see difficulty as an opportunity to worship Allah, and therefore, exhibit calmness and praise Allah for the chance to come closer to Him. Allah even mentions in the Quran, in Surah Baqarah,

"O you who have believed, seek help through patience and prayer. Indeed, Allah is with the patient." [Al-Quran; 2:153]

This further emphasizes the importance of patience. We all already know the importance of prayer. It is one of those things that we must do no matter what situation we are in, and in this ayah, Allah is mentioning patience alongside prayer, which shows just how important patience is in our deen. So, it is very important to be patient especially during times of crisis.

This pandemic has everyone cooped up in their own shell. This awful virus has acted as both a test for some and punishment for others. A lot of people are bored and have found nothing to do with all the extra time, which is why I personally think that Allah has tested me to see what I will do with it. Nevertheless, we should be grateful to Allah and accept this blessing and make the most of it, because we never know when Allah will take it away from us. In order to spend all this free time, we should try doing new things or learn something new. It is easier to take part in more extracurriculars because everything has gone virtual. Though many people prefer things to be more hands-on and in person, we must follow the pandemic protocols in order to keep ourselves and our friends and family safe. And finally, we must be patient and pray to Allah to guide us through these troubling times. There are many things to do even if we are all at home, and I am sure that after your next boring webinar, you will have time to do something fun.

Young Muslim Voices

2nd Place: Emira Syeda-Ali
Home School, Gaithersburg, MD

Al-Khaliq says in Al-Qur'an:

"Indeed, We created man from a sperm-drop mixture that We may try him..." [Al-Quran; 76:2]

In life are tests for believers. What about COVID-19? Some say it is *al-azaab* (a punishment); some say it is *ibtalaa* (a test). Clearly Allah (SWT) says everything in life is a test, including COVID-19. However, if we do not take this test seriously, it will turn into *al-azaab*. The same goes with *ad-dunya* (this world)- if we do not productively use *As-saa'ah* (the time), *ad-dunya* will turn into *al-azaab*. On the day of judgment, we will be asked how productive we were during COVID-19. This essay discusses the ideal mindset of believers, and how to turn that into productive action during COVID-19.

Let us commence with the mindset of believers. Allah (SWT) willed, in *ad-dunya*, hardships strike everyone. For non-believers, they are inconveniences that block them from proceeding with life. For believers, they are instances of rest and remembrance, promising rewards, and indications of reparation and expiation of sins. Regardless of the size of the harm, it carries *bashirhu-bimaghfira* (glad tidings of forgiveness) and higher ranks in Jannah. The righteous are pleased when hardship afflicts them, seeing it as tokens of Allah (SWT)'s *maghfira-wa rahma* (forgiveness and mercy). Anas (RA) narrates, RasulAllah (SAWS) said:

"I am amazed by the believer. Verily, Allah does not decree anything for the believer except what is good for him." [Musnad Ahmad]

The *Hubul-Allah* (most beloved to Allah) *Al-Anbiyaa* (the prophets) faced the toughest tests. It stands to reason the believers will be tested too. Why do believers suffer the most, while others enjoy *ad-dunya*, and how sure are we, these are not punishments for them? Abu Hurayrah (RA) narrates, RasulAllah (SAWS) said:

"He whom Allah intends good; He makes him to suffer from some affliction." [Sahih Al-Bukhari]

For comparable tests, why do believers get rewarded, while others get punished? If believers are patient and submit to Allah (SWT)'s will, they will be rewarded for submission and the test. As Imam Ibn Hajar said:

"The sahih ahadith are clear in the rewards are recorded once affliction strikes a Muslim. As for patience and acceptance, they are virtues for a person may get additional rewards over those for the affliction." [Ibn Hajar Al- Asqalani; Fath Al-Bari]

Ibn Masud (RA) narrates, RasulAllah (SAWS) said:

"No Muslim is afflicted with any harm, but that Allah will remove his sins as the leaves of a tree fall down." [Sahih Al-Bukhari]

The mindset of believers involves productive action during COVID-19. Doing our part to prevent COVID-19 from spreading is the straightforward action. Doctors promote personal hygiene to limit spread, especially washing hands for twenty-seconds. Islam encouraged personal hygiene for centuries. Ashari (RA) narrates, RasulAllah (SAWS) said:

"Cleanliness is half of faith." [Sahih Muslim]

Performing Wudu removes germs, dust and diseases. Approximately five hundred to one-thousand bacteria species live on skin according to a study. Performing Wudu washes away potentially pathogenic germs on skin. How can we prove Wudu's benefits? Britain reported COVID-19 cases coming from Britain's Muslim neighborhoods were lower than other neighborhoods. Furthermore, there are no Muslim-majority countries with leading COVID-19 cases. I am certain Muslims perform ablution before praying. Occasionally, we can be unmindful. COVID-19 gives us time to perfect our Wudu. Insha'Allah, after COVID-19 is mitigated we will get better at it.

We as Muslims need to encourage everyone to do the right thing, even if it is uncomfortable. This brings up face masks, usually uncomfortable to wear, but effective in protecting people. Staying home and social distancing abolish harm. AbuHurayrah (RA) narrates, RasulAllah (SAWS) said:

"...removing a harmful object from the road is a charity." [Sahih Al-Bukhari]

In another Hadith, Anas (RA) narrates, Rasul Allah (SAWS) said:

"None of you truly believes until he loves for his brother (or for his neighbor), what he loves for himself." [Sunan Ibn Majah]

Scientists are trying to contain COVID-19, but they need us to wear masks, maintain social distancing or stay home, to protect ourselves and the rest of society.

Before COVID-19, many claimed to be busy to earn *hasanat* (good deeds). COVID-19 allowed us to have idle time. Allah (SWT) will ask us what we did with our time, especially during COVID-19. Time is finite, and it is imperative we use it *Fee-Sabilillah* (in the path of Allah). Allah (SWT) swears by time in Al-Qur'an:

"By time; indeed, mankind is in loss. Except for those who have believed and done righteous deeds and advised each other to truth and advised each other to patience." [Al-Quran; 103:3]

Now we should turn to Al-Ghaffar with *istighfar* (asking for forgiveness). Ibn Abbas (RA) narrates, RasulAllah (SAWS) said,

"If anyone constantly seeks pardon (from Allah), Allah will appoint for him a way out of every distress and a relief from every anxiety and will provide sustenance for him from where he expects not." [Sunan Abi Dawud]

Before COVID-19, many barely spent time with their families. Now with more time at home, spending quality time with our household is easy. Islam mandates being good with our families. Aisha (RA) narrates, RasulAllah (SAWS) said:

"The best of you is he who is best to his family..." [Sunan At-Tirmidhi]

Now is the time to spend quality time with our families and make everlasting memories. Otherwise, we will regret it later. After COVID-19 is mitigated we will cherish As-Saa'ah we spent with our family.

We can use idle time to aid others. Ibn Umar (RA) narrates, RasulAllah (SAWS) said:

"Whoever fulfilled the needs of his brother, Allah will fulfill his needs; whoever brought his (Muslim) brother out of a discomfort, Allah will bring him out of the discomforts of the Day of Resurrection." [Sahih Al-Bukhari]

We should determine which neighbors need help shopping since COVID-19 made it difficult for many to shop safely. For those who cannot afford food we can donate food, money, or participate in food drives. For those isolated community members, engage in virtual conversations. These examples should motivate us to spend our idle time *Fee-sabilillah*.

In conclusion, COVID-19 is *ibtalaa* for believers that we must pass; otherwise, it becomes *al-azaab*. During COVID-19, Allah (SWT) has given us many blessings. It made us comprehend that we should not take anything for granted, because Allah (SWT) can seize it within seconds. COVID-19 taught us that Allah (SWT) is *Rabbul-A'lamin* (Lord of the worlds); we only turn to Him for guidance. We learned to sacrifice our comfort to protect others, regardless of how uncomfortable that is. COVID-19 showed us that time flies, but if we use it productively, we can earn *hasanat*. Imam Ash-Shafi'i's poetic reminder:

"Be optimistic when destiny decrees,

do not despair due to events nights past,
for the event of Ad-Dunya are not to last,

and be a person strong in the face of calamities,

and let your nature be of your kindness and honesty."

['Let the days go forth' by Imam Ash-Shafi'i; translated by Ammar Al-Shukry]

3rd Place: Syed Ahnaf Hossain
ADAMS Center, Herndon, VA

Patience is crucial. Patience has always been crucial. But it has never been more crucial than now. Corona virus has turned our lives upside down, inside out, and backwards. It forced us into our homes and forced us to stay in our homes since March 16th. After nine months, with the world at war with an enemy we cannot see, people are desperate to go back outside. But we cannot and we must continue to stay indoors. At this point, we as Muslims should have something that other people are now willing to let go of to get outside: patience.

But there is more to it than just having patience. While we all as humanity are suffering, we have something that the disbelievers do not have. We have hope of Allah (SWT) to forgive us and reward us. This is close to what the Qur'an says:

"...If you should be suffering - so, are they suffering as you are suffering, but you expect from Allah that which they expect not. And Allah is ever Knowing and Wise." [Al-Quran; 4:104]

With this mindset, we should try and attain higher levels of reward by doing more good deeds while stuck in our homes during the pandemic. It is very easy to acquire good deeds to your account. Simple statements, such as *'SubhanAllah'* or *'Astaghfirullah'*, can give so much reward, as long as it is sincere.

One aspect we should focus on is the grief people are feeling during these times. The sudden losses of so many loved ones- it is something we cannot bear. But those who had Iman and passed away with COVID-19 have been given something that we have not been given. The Prophet Muhammad (SAWS) said,

"Every Muslim who dies of plague is credited with martyrdom." [Sahih Al-Bukhari]

Allah does not punish or test a people unless they are committing sins. He says in the Qur'an:

"That is because Allah would not change a favor which He had bestowed upon a people until they change what is within themselves. And indeed, Allah is Hearing and Knowing." [Al-Quran; 8:53]

The corona virus is not only a punishment or a test, but also a blessing. It gave us the ability to give importance to the things we neglected, such as praying on time. It let those of us who were busy become free and be there with those whom we couldn't be with before. It should also make us aware of the power and punishment of Allah (SWT) and encourage us to avoid sin.

So, with that, we know Muslims are an opportunistic people, and in shaa Allah, we can make the most of this pandemic.

Special Recognition – Essay: Hafiza Chowdhury ADAMS, Herndon, VA

The world has been plunged into chaos. Unrelenting fear and distress and sorrow—that is what the coronavirus pandemic has brought with it. Many people are grieving and in pain at this very moment. This may be a test, but it may well be a punishment. How does anyone know what it truly is? It does not matter, anyway. All that matters right now is how people choose to handle the situation and whether they decide to follow the rules and try to help others.

There are several ways that people's minds respond to the current situation of the world and this pandemic. Some think it may be a punishment because of the horrible things some humans have done. Others believe it is a test, maybe because Allah tests those He loves. Many more people simply think that the whole of 2020 is a year gone wrong, and there is nothing more to the pandemic other than it being a pandemic.

The coronavirus is a disease that has affected many people, sweeping through the world like a tsunami, washing away lives, breaking families, and leaving destruction in its wake. Some people have lost their source of income due to being forced to stay at home. It has killed many people worldwide. Starting in Wuhan, China, it spread to Europe and then to other continents and countries, until the whole world was affected and awash with loss. More than 77.5 million people have caught it, and more than 1.4 million people have died after contracting this disease. Tens of thousands of families have lost a beloved member or relative to this disease.

With all of this going on, it is only natural that several people's mental health has crumbled like rocks on a cliff's edge. It is perfectly normal to feel down and lose confidence, and even easier to let go of hope. Worldwide, there are people who are struggling with this virus just as much as you may be. Some are affected less, and some more. Whether all of this is a punishment or a test, it does not matter. We are all in this together, locked in this battle until we can figure out how to end it. There is no harm in trying to find out what this truly is, but there is no gain either. Instead, there are other ways to face this situation.

It may be difficult to hang onto a determined, positive mindset, just as difficult as it is to hold sand in our hands without a grain seeping through. Despite this, we still must try. We must encourage others to stay hopeful and keep going. We should warn them to be careful and reassure them that it will be alright. Positivity is something that is hard for some to come by in these times, and now more than ever, it may be worth more than gold. Yet hope costs nothing, and it is important to spread it whenever and however we can.

Checking on friends, family, and neighbors is also something everyone should try to do in this trying time, if they have the ability, and to help their companions if they need it. It is especially vital that we maintain social distance and wear masks, not for solely our own safety, but for everyone around us when we go out. It may be helpful to remind those we see to wear a mask when they do not wear one in public. Social distancing is a major component needed to reach recovery and start rebuilding. We should stay a minimum of six feet away from others when we go to the store or to work. Lend a helping hand to those that need it. Try to ease their stress and be a ray of light in this dark.

The last thing is dua. Dua is the key element and one of our few hopes for a solution and an end to this pandemic. We should make as much dua as we can, for our friends and family, for this pandemic to be over, and for everything to be okay once again. Dua may very well be the key to solving all this, if all else continues to fail. It may unlock the solution with a simple click, as if the answer to all of this had been hiding behind a real lock.

Despite everything going on, even with the current state of the world and the death surrounding us, it does not matter if this is a test or a punishment. What matters is that we keep praying and making dua. Remember that while it may be easy to despair in these lightless times, stars cannot shine without darkness. What matters is that we make sure our loved ones stay healthy and safe, and that we make sure we keep anyone we encounter safe by wearing a mask and staying socially distanced from them. The coronavirus pandemic, just like all other major historical events, will lose momentum. It will slow and come to an end, and the world will bring itself back up stronger, just as it has before. Everything will be fine. All we have to do is persevere and pray.

Young Muslim Voices

Special Recognition – Speech: Khadijah Samiya
Eleanor Roosevelt High School, Greenbelt, MD

Asalamalykum,

Coronavirus! The virus that changed how we see the world from now on. Remember those days when we would go to the mall with our friends? That wedding with more than 500 guests? I'm sure you've been to one if you're desi. 2020 sure is over, but it isn't forgotten. Our lives have forever been changed. After the coronavirus hit, the world wasn't sure when everything's going to go back to normal again. It took me a while, but I have made my own way of coping. Even though I couldn't visit my extended family in person, I became close with my immediate family. With my extended family, there's your phone, Facetime, Skype, Hangouts and many more. I tried my best and am still trying to make my mindset at peace. I try to clear my mind at some points of the day to reflect on how my day was and how to make the next day better. Especially during this pandemic, we should focus more on ourselves and others around us.

Prophet Muhammad encouraged Muslims to keep strong family ties. The Quran inspires Muslims to be generous to kin and treat the elderly with compassion. It's important to keep good relations with everyone, especially family and friends. There would be regular weekly events and gatherings, but it soon stopped. All the hugging and shaking hands stopped in the second week of March. I remember March 2020 like it was yesterday. It truly made everyone confused and curious about what happened and when things would go back to normal. Now, we're learning to adapt to different ways. It's very important for us to have a good mindset and make sure that we can learn from this pandemic to reach out to others that are in need and who we haven't talked to. I truly believe that this pandemic has made everyone realize the true meaning of family and friends and what it means to be together. Did we get sick of each other? Yes, but did it make us stronger? Yes. Reflecting on your day makes the next day even better, so I think that to make us even more productive the next day, we should see today and the other days.

HIGH SCHOOL | LEVEL 6

Topic:

Some say the coronavirus pandemic is a punishment, some say it is a test. Either way, what should the mindset of a Muslim be during a global event of this scale and how should that translate into productive action?

1st Place: Jannah A. Nassar
River Hill High School, Clarksville, MD

Due to the COVID-19 pandemic, 2020 brought some very difficult challenges including a worldwide shutdown leaving millions of people unemployed, hundreds of thousands of students struggling to learn in a virtual environment, hundreds of businesses forced to shut down, and one US economy facing the largest shrink since the Great Depression in the 1930s. As Muslims we must use these as a reminder to strive for Al-Akhira and have one common mindset: having trust in Allah (SWT).

This is a mindset that can be described as tawakkul. Tawakkul means having trust in Allah (SWT) and taking action to achieve the desired outcomes. For instance, if one would like to receive a specific grade on an exam, if they study and put in effort, the grade they receive is up to Allah (SWT) as He does what is best for them. In this case you took action and now must trust that Allah (SWT) will satisfy your needs.

Tawakkul is a large part of Islam and is mentioned multiple times in the Quran, stressing its importance. One specific ayah is in Surah At-Talaq which translates to

"And will provide for him from where he does not expect. And whoever relies upon Allah - then He is sufficient for him. Indeed, Allah will accomplish His purpose. Allah has already set for everything a [decreed] extent." [Al- Quran; 65:3]

By strengthening your tawakkul, you place yourself in the correct mindset to accept any challenges and allow yourself to take action to get where you need to go. For instance, if you have an exam, having tawakkul means that you spend time studying and rely on Allah (SWT) to satisfy your needs.

In Islam, tawakul is not optional but rather a requirement to strengthen our relationship with Allah (SWT). Surah Al-Ma'idah, verse number 23 translates to,

"...And upon Allah rely, if you should be believers." [Al-Quran; 5:23]

A true believer will never doubt Allah's (SWT) plan for him. This allows one to accept challenges much easier because they can be certain that Allah (SWT) only does what is best for them.

Now, how exactly do you put your trust in Allah (SWT)? Trust is not a physical object and for that reason it's often difficult for people to measure. However, productive action items that increase one's tawakkul include saying Alhamdulillah, making du'aa, having a strong relationship with the Quran, and using the five daily prayers as a reminder.

First, many people put their trust in Allah (SWT) by saying Alhamdulillah regardless of the outcomes. For instance, if one does not receive the grade he or she hoped for on an exam, say Alhamdulillah, let go of the outcome and trust that this is part of Allah's (SWT) plan for you. Oftentimes, in our day and age, teenagers forget that no matter the amount of hard work you put in, nothing will happen unless Allah (SWT) wills for it. So, saying Alhamdulliah acts as a reminder to praise Allah (SWT) and trust His plan regardless of the outcomes desired.

Another productive action item would include making du'aa. Du'aa is one of the greatest acts of worship and a large component of having a strong tawakkul. As Rooh Thair from Yaqeen Institute explains, *"Du'aa is the weapon of the believer, but it's only as strong as the one who recognizes how to best use it to maximize its benefit. We often make the mistake of limiting our du'a to our own limited perception. Don't be afraid to ask Allah- He moves mountains for those who ask.*

Hence, tawakkul leads to a life of confidence and certainty." Consequently, dua'a is required to provide confidence and further help one place his or her trust in Allah (SWT).

Third, having a strong relationship with the Quran is essential to having strong tawakkul and the correct mindset. A close relationship with the Quran allows one to better understand his or her deen, form a stronger relationship with Allah (SWT), and better understand why placing one's trust in Allah (SWT) is essential.

Finally, another important way to get into the correct mindset is to use the five daily prayers as a reminder. Allah (SWT) gives us the opportunity to converse with Him five times a day. As stated by Yaqeen Institute, one should "reflect on the words we recite in every unit of prayer" allowing [you] to unburden [your] hearts and minds. Additionally, "prayer is a means to stay on course, gain rewards and forgiveness, and to increase one's faith and tawakkul." Thus, a productive action item to form the correct mindset.

Not only is tawakul required in Islam, but it's extremely beneficial to us as Muslims. One major benefit of strong tawakkul is that no matter what hardship one faces, the trust in Allah (SWT) allows them to remain strong when facing these difficulties. Surah Al-Baqarah verse number 286 translates to

"Allah does not charge a soul except [with that within] its capacity." [Al-Quran; 2:286]

Tawakkul provides a mindset in which you can feel safer knowing Allah (SWT) will satisfy your needs. It's the mercy of Allah (SWT) that tells us our responsibility is limited and allows us to trust Allah (SWT) will get us through difficulties. Additionally, by trusting Allah (SWT), one can become humbler knowing that all things are in the hands of Allah (SWT).

So regardless of whether the challenges brought on by the pandemic were blessings or punishments, Muslims must have a common mindset of having strong tawakkul.

So, next time you face a challenge, remember you will come out stronger from the test, be rewarded in the akhira, and use it as a reminder that this life is not what we should be striving for.

Young Muslim Voices

2nd Place: Omar Ali
Home School, Lanham, MD

The pandemic has put the world to a stop. There hasn't been, in recent history, a more dangerous and contagious disease. The last deadly plague was the Ebola outbreak in 2014. Although the Ebola outbreak was fatal, Covid-19 is much more contagious than the Ebola outbreak. With it being contagious, this sent most of the world into a lockdown, where nobody can leave the home unless for services. Everything was sent to a halt, and work and school were continued in the home. This was the new norm for the world this year. Some people may say that it is a punishment from Allah or a test from Allah. This virus is a living thing and Allah sent this. Even though, alhamdulilah, we live in a generation where there are so many technological advancements and medicine has evolved so much, Allah gave us a reminder that He is the greatest and the tech and medicine we have today couldn't even combat this virus. A virus that we cannot see from the naked eye. We as human beings believe that we are the greatest, but we are scared of a virus that an advanced microscope can only see. As seen in textual evidence, Allah cannot be stopped. For the people of 'Aad, Allah sent an angel that only lifted one wing, and the whole town went down and got destroyed. Therefore, Allah gave us a reminder that He is the greatest.

Allah says,

"Corruption has appeared throughout the land and sea by [reason of] what the hands of people have earned so He [i.e., Allah] may let them taste part of [the consequence of] what they have done that perhaps they will return [to righteousness]." [Al-Quran; 30:41]

Allah tells us that we have so much sin and corruption in his land and to give a reminder, have a taste for what we have done. Yes, I and you should be positive when things like this take place, but we should also be aware of Allah's greatness and quickness on how fast He can make the creation become belittled.

Our mindset should be that this pandemic gave us a chance to come back to Allah and ask for forgiveness for what you and I have done. Some people may have a mindset where it does not affect the young, it only affects the old and the disabled. This mindset is probably one of the worst mindsets people can have. The reason for this is because most young people have older loved ones that they cherish who are very vulnerable to this and if they are affected, they might die (may God forbid). With that being said, the young people can affect the old and the young can be affected by sadness because of the loss of their older loved ones (may God forbid). With the lockdown taking place in this country, people tried to be in their best hygiene possible because they do not want to get affected. Medical professionals recommend washing hands for at least 20 seconds every time when coming home and not to touch your face. They don't understand that this may be a punishment of Allah and they don't tell you to make tawbah to Allah. Imam Hassan Al-Basari says,

"If the people have been inflicted by hardship or difficulty, it is from the wrath of Allah. Do not try to prevent the wrath of Allah through precautions."

Therefore, the mindset cannot be anything except that it is repenting to Allah.

One can repent to Allah by reading the Quran, praying salah, praying sunnah salah, waking up to pray the night prayer, etc. Allah is Ar-Rahman, the Most Merciful. Forgiveness can be answered and rectified by the will of Allah. Because the world is in a lockdown. There is more time being taken. Allah gave us a plague which was a reminder and a punishment and a time to beg for Allah's mercy. Therefore, prayers should be longer than usual, reading the Quran should be more often, and dhikr should be more often as well. Allah loves the one who forgives. Although we may try to seek repentance from Allah, and this problem has occurred to me and others, is that we go back to the sin. The best thing to do is to seek repentance and try your best to abolish that sin. We are the children of Adam (AS) and we do make sins. But that is what we do when we commit that sin.

Overall, the pandemic gave a shock to the world, and it put the world at a standstill. Allah put out a virus so small that it can't be seen with a naked eye, and it put everybody in their homes and lost some loved ones. This calamity is a reminder that Allah is the greatest. This calamity is also a reminder that Allah is the most merciful and we should repent to Allah. So, therefore, this is my take on the situation that we live in now.

3rd Place: Raakin Kabir
ADAMS Center, Sterling, VA

Throughout history, lamentable conditions are easily seen. Simply considering World War II, the Black Death, and the coronavirus should suffice. All these events seem to have no overall benefit to the world and would have been better off not existing in the first place. One might question the reason for such an event in the first place. Why would Allah (SWT) allow this? Or what good reason is there for it? Oftentimes, this prompts individuals to question Allah (SWT) and (perhaps) lose faith. This is known as the Problem of Evil, a philosophical question regarding the seeming evil in the world in conjunction with an omnibenevolent, monotheistic belief of a deity. The problem will be tackled from both a philosophical route and an Islamic route. The philosophical route deals with the seeming contradiction between benevolence and evil, and the Islamic route examines the fundamentals of the doctrine. Contrary to what individuals might believe, an omnibenevolent, omniscient, and omnipotent being and suffering in the world are not contradictory. In addition, unbeknownst to the individuals, the Problem of Evil is already addressed within Islam. One simply needs to understand the fundamentals of Islam. What does it mean to be a Muslim? What is the definition of a Muslim? Through such questioning, one can realize that for a Muslim, the omnibenevolent nature of Allah (SWT) is not contradictory with the sufferings of this world (such as the coronavirus). Suffering is a necessary aspect as it pertains to Allah's (SWT) plan (as a test). This realization should prompt a Muslim to fulfill their duty as a follower of Islam, adhering to the doctrine.

As aforementioned, The Problem of Evil regards the apparent contradiction between an omnibenevolent, omnipotent, and omniscient being and evil in the world. The basic argument is: if God knows about all of the evil in the world, knows how to eliminate/

prevent it, is powerful enough to prevent it, and yet does not prevent it, He must not be perfectly good. *[James R Beebee; Logical Problem of Evil]*

A counterargument to this is if it is possible for God to have a morally sufficient reason for allowing evil (example given later), then it is possible for God to have the aforementioned qualities and allow apparent evil. Due to the possibility of a morally sufficient reason, proof must be given for lack of morally sufficient reason. To consider an example of this, consider someone who hears that a child unwillingly undergoes pain, but did not hear that the child went through a flu shot. Naturally, the individual would consider this a moral evil and respond as such. However, upon hearing that the child had a flu shot, a rational person would shift their attitude from angry/distressed to calm and understanding. In the same manner, were God to have a morally sufficient reason for allowing evil and suffering, the reason would be akin to the individual in the flu shot scenario. Hence, evil does not necessarily contradict the nature of God.

However, some may not be convinced by this argument, as one could argue that the argument appeals to the *possibility* of a morally sufficient reason. To prove a lack of explanation for each and every evil would not suffice, as there is no way to know if a potential explanation is true or not. In that case, there is another way to approach this problem. To construct such an argument, an important distinction should be made. Evil can be divided into two categories: natural evil and moral evil. Moral evils are evils that result from the intentions or negligence of a moral agent (e.g., human), such as murder and lying. In contrast, natural evils are evils that do not result from such, like hurricanes and earthquakes. *[Todd Calder; The Concept of Evil]* Coronavirus hence is considered to be a natural evil. Regarding moral evil (like World War II), one argument that could be used pertains to free will. Alvin Plantinga, a contemporary philosopher of religion writes,

"God could not eliminate much of the evil and suffering in this world without thereby eliminating the greater good of having created persons with free will with whom he could have relationships and who are able to love one another and do good deeds." [James R Beebee; Logical Problem of Evil]

Hence, because people have free will, evil is allowed. However, what about natural evil? Free will does not seem to pertain to natural evil as they appear unrelated. One argument used, however, is that *"natural evils provide us with a knowledge of evil which makes our free choices more significant than they would otherwise be, and so our free will is more valuable"*. To give an example of this, consider a mother who loses her child in an earthquake. The child could have been saved if the rescue workers were more physically adept. The mother now faces the choice of lashing out/insulting the rescue workers or to slowly accept the situation and forgive. Because the mother faces a much more difficult choice, the significance of the free will increases heavily and hence becomes more valuable. This argument is closely related to Islamic belief of life, as Allah (SWT) tests us via suffering, and that suffering allows potential for greater moral virtue.

The fundamentals of the doctrine of Islam also address the Problem of Evil. To start, considering the meaning of life on Earth should suffice. Allah (SWT) tells us that life on Earth is a moral test. The Qur'an states,

"[He] who created death and life to test you [as to] which of you is best in deed - and He is the Exalted in Might, the Forgiving..." [Al-Quran; 67:2]

As life is a test, this implies that there will be a struggle to choose the morally good. Due to the implication of struggle, some failure is to be expected (hence moral evil). However, what should a Muslim do in times of affliction? Allah (SWT) clearly tells us to adhere to the belief in Him (faith). As the Qur'an states,

"And We will surely test you with something of fear and hunger and a loss of wealth and lives and fruits, but give good tidings to the patient, Who, when disaster strikes them, say, "Indeed we belong to Allah, and indeed to Him we will return."" *[Al-Quran; 2:155-156]*

With the establishment of the mindset developed via the arguments above, what should a Muslim *do* in times of serious suffering? As discussed, tragedies like the coronavirus, which has yielded devastating impacts globally, should not be misunderstood as an unjust calamity from Allah (SWT).

Suffering is part of the test of life and those who succeed reap many benefits. This change in mindset should result in some intrinsic motivation for action. What can a Muslim who observes suffering do? Suffering in general offers opportunities to a Muslim. To aid the suffering is a morally virtuous choice. As Prophet Muhammed (SAWS) says,

"'Whoever relieves a Muslim of some worldly distress, Allah will relieve him of some of the distress of the Day of Resurrection, and whoever conceals (the faults of) a Muslim, Allah will conceal him (his faults) in this world and the Day of Resurrection." [Sunan Ibn Majah]

Hence, it would be productive for a Muslim to aid others. The manner in which one should aid is dependent on the individual.

Suffering occurs in every historical period and can evoke strong emotions that make one question Allah (SWT). Indeed, it is so apparent that huge debates have arisen from observations of the world, formally constituted as the Problem of Evil. Some have unfortunately conformed to one-sided speculations and made up their mind without regarding the other side. Upon a closer inspection upon the arguments and Islam, it becomes quite evident that there is justified reason for evil. A Muslim should take a closer inspection for themselves to strengthen their mindset and become more reasoned in thinking and defending their religion. Indeed, Allah (SWT) promotes reason in the following verse:

"And whatever thing you [people] have been given - it is [only for] the enjoyment of worldly life and its adornment. And what is with Allah is better and more lasting; so, will you not use reason?" [Al-Quran; 28:60]

Upon using reason, how a Muslim should react to suffering should become clear, as life on Earth is a test. The most difficult test, but also the most fulfilling.

2022

Islam and Mental Health

ELEMENTARY SCHOOL | LEVEL 1

Topic:

Write a letter to your loved one describing a time when you had a problem, how it made you feel, and how you handled it.

1st Place: Zaynab Mehmood
MCC Sunday School, Silver Spring, MD

Assalamualaikum Baba,

Second grade has been wonderful, but I had one issue. A classmate bullied me. People solve problems with their brain, but I add in my heart. Allah puts Iman (faith) in our hearts. The Quran was revealed on Muhammad's (SAWS) heart! The heart communicates with the brain. The brain commands the body to solve problems with positivity. The Quran says

"Our Lord, let not our hearts deviate after You have guided us..." [Al-Quran; 3:8]

For the bullying, I decided to follow the 3 sections of my heart method. The 3 sections: first turn to Allah, second share your feelings and finally look for solutions and take action. Let's explore!

Section 1 is to turn to Allah. As a Muslim, I surrender and submit to Allah. When a problem arrives, I make dua for Allah to handle the situation. Allah says in the Quran,

"Call upon Me; I will respond to you." [Al-Quran; 40:60]

That is amazing.

Section 2 is to share your feelings with loved ones. I share with my parents and siblings; they are solution oriented. Bullying makes me feel stressed and disheartened. Keeping my feelings inside will affect my mental health. My mind and heart are like gardens, I want flowers, not weeds!

Section 3 is to look for solutions and take action. I told my teacher, and she moved my seat away from the bully. When the bully was mean, I said, "Stop, I don't appreciate that." I learned to solve the problem.

In conclusion, I hope you enjoyed my heart method. Mental health is an important topic. I am committed to a growth mindset. I will not let my brain and heart feel depressed. Allah loves me and I love Him!

Love!

2nd Place: Noora Khan
Home School, Reston, VA

Dear Ms. Aziza,

I want to tell you that something happened last month. I had a big problem. I was excited to go to my friend's birthday party. But it was at an ice-skating rink, and it was my first time skating.

At first, I was holding on to the wall. I was feeling frustrated and scared. Another girl slipped and fell on me. Ouch!

My friend's dad came over to help me. He told me to put my feet in a little, bend my knees, and waddle like a duck. I practiced those steps, and I was able to let go of the wall! After the party I asked my mom to sign me up for ice-skating lessons. They start this weekend!

I learned to never give up and Allah will help you.

Love.

3rd Place: Tasfia Amin
Park International School and College, Dhaka

Dear Rufaida,

How are you? I hope everything is going well for you. How are your parents doing? My family and I are doing well as well. I really missed you. You know How much I love you. I know you love me, which is why I share all my secrets, joys and the most beautiful moments of my life with you. So now I am going to send you a letter in which I describe a moment when I was suffering and also having so many difficult situations that I will go through all of the health problems, and how I overcame from there. I will tell you about every single thing that happened to me. Last month I was feeling really unwell, and I had a fever of 104 degrees, and I was vomiting a lot. My parents were worried about me and took me to the doctor. The doctor suggested that I get blood tests done. The report came in the morning and stated that I was a dengue positive patient who needed to be admitted to the hospital straight away. According to the diagnosis my platelet level was very low so I couldn't eat properly, and I was really afraid. My parents were crying so hard. The doctor gave me different types of medicines. My parents informed everyone that my platelet count had dropped to around 22,000 and that I would have to have blood transfusions to raise my platelet count. At the time, it was an unexpected situation for me. All of my family members including my dad and uncle were at my side, and after a few days I began to eat something, and my platelet level started to rise. And I must say it was truly Allah's mercy. My mother constantly encouraged me to pray to Allah to get out of that problem. Everyone prayed for my fast recovery. My mother constantly encouraged me to pray to Allah to get out of that problem. Everyone prayed for my fast recovery. My mother told me that Allah had saved me from the condition.

I felt strong and lively after 8 days. Rufaidah, you called me, but I couldn't talk to you on those days. Rufaida, you are such a kind, loving, and friendly person. I felt so lucky that I have a friend like you as a best buddy. I used to recite duas for my recovery at the time. These duas are quite good for healing someone quickly.

Allahumma inni audhubika min-al barasi, wal junooni, wal juzaami, wa min sayyil asqaam. (Oh Allah, I seek Your refuge from leprosy, insanity, mutilation, and from all serious illness.)
[Sunan Abi Dawud]

Rufaidah, pray for me. Love you so much, take care.

Your lovely.

Special Recognition – Essay: Rafia Khanam Raha
Park International School and College, Dhaka

Dear Fazlous Uncle,

How are you? I hope that you are fine. I am also well with the blessing of the almighty. Did you know that before the last half-yearly exam I was very sick? It was a sunny day, and everything was fine. I was playing with my puppet and toys. My father was in his office, and mom also went to a nearby market to shop. Suddenly I got exhausted and felt uncomfortable. To get relief from this uneasiness, I went to my bed. But a severe headache started. It was the most painful experience that I have ever experienced. Afraid of the pain I called my mom to come back home as soon as possible. Mom rushed home after getting my call. She then informed my father immediately. Hearing this news my father also rushed home. In the meantime, I fainted. But as I was unconscious, I could not realize where I was going. After regaining consciousness, I found myself in a hospital bed. Doctors and nurses had surrounded me along with my parents. My teachers and relatives were also praying for me. Opening my eyes, I found myself in my mom's lap. My parents were tearing at that time. Both of them were kissing my cheeks. The doctor told them that there was an imminent danger, but timely intervention saved my life.

Please keep me in your prayers.

With best wishes,
Your niece

Young Muslim Voices

Special Recognition – Speech: Ridimaa Alam
Park International School and College, Dhaka

Dear Cousin,

I hope you are fine. Glad to know that you got good marks in your exams. I heard that you are a little bit upset about the English subject. I am sharing my story that may help you to overcome that. When I was three years old, I visited Malaysia with my parents. I couldn't speak in English, and I even didn't understand it. I saw lots of children playing and talking in English. I wanted to talk and play with them. I felt very lonely and bad. So, I played with a little cat. Later I asked my parents about English. They said, "English is the most used and spoken language around the world. Learning English will increase the chances to get a job, participate in discussion and improve networking skills."

Then I decided to learn English. I started to watch English content from YouTube. I watched different cartoons namely Peppa Pig, Barbie, Doraemon, Hello Kitty; English rhymes, poems, songs, stories, and everything that I found in English. At first, I made a lot of videos, talked in front of the mirror, talked with Google and my parents in English. I was so happy and encouraged. At school, my teachers are regularly helping me to nurture my English skills. So don't be upset, don't be shy; just keep trying to learn.

I want you to visit my place. We will enjoy our vacation together.

Take care,
Your loving sister

ELEMENTARY SCHOOL | LEVEL 2

Topic:

How do the problems you face affect your mind and what can you do to stay positive while facing these problems? How did the Prophet of Islam (SAW) teach you to stay positive while in a situation like this?

1st Place: Mariam Ali Souleymane
Homeschooling, Champaign-Urbana, IL

"Problems are like washing machines. They twist us, spin us, and knock us around... in the end, we come out cleaner and better than before."-Madeleine Wickham

The quote above explains that problems can help us improve ourselves by adding more experiences through our daily basis to help make ourselves stronger. But there are many different kinds of problems- some of them can harm our mental health which is not good because it can cause illnesses like depression. Many people suffer depression because of social media and bully-like actions toward them. It will be best for us as Muslims to learn about what the Prophet (SAWS) and Allah advised to help situate our problems.

Problems can affect our minds in so many ways, so they may be different from your siblings or friends. The effect they have on my mind will be a fixed mindset when the mind becomes negative, and you start to be a coward while improving your homework, projects, and others. But I got over it. But I don't get over the problem. I get lost in thought about how I could've solved or prevented the problem. Other times if it is unsolvable, I think about what we could've done if there wasn't a problem. But Allah says: *"Indeed, with hardship [will be] ease." [Al-Quran; 94:6]*

Staying positive while facing problems can be hard most of the time because they can be pretty big and frustrating, they can put a lot of pressure on us. To stay positive while facing problems I talk to someone who is older than me and that I can trust to talk about my problems. After a long talk, I feel like a huge weight has lifted off my shoulders. Sometimes I will read a book that makes my mind start to feel positive again. But then again, everyone's methods will be different from everyone else's.

"And be patient, for indeed, Allah does not allow to be lost the reward of those who do good." [Al-Quran; 11:115] The ayah above explains that Allah will reward you through your hardships if you put trust in Him. As people go through problems the best solution is patience and perseverance. I learned it while we do Seerah at school. Prophet Muhammad (SAWS) was always patient and put his belief in Allah every time. He even told his sahabah that the Muslims who suffer will get an unbelievable amount of reward.

"Wondrous is the affair of the believer for there is good for him in every matter and this is not the case with anyone except the believer. If he is happy, then he thanks Allah and thus there is good for him, and if he is harmed, then he shows patience and thus there is good for him." [Sahih Muslim]

"Problems aren't stop signs they are guidelines"- Robert Schuller Problems can help us and sometimes be frustrating, we can use Islam to help.

Young Muslim Voices

2nd Place: Raidah Islam
Al-Huda School, College Park, MD

There are some problems that I face almost every day in my life that ruin my mood or make me feel sad. It is difficult to stay positive, but I try my best to stay calm even though I am angry. The Quran and the Prophet Muhammad (SAWS) has taught me how to stay positive when I face my problems.

Some of the problems that I face include not wanting to do Hifz, not wanting to clean the house, and brother bothering me. I try to learn how to handle these situations so that I can be happy. Islam teaches us that during stressful situations we should always stay calm and be patient. We should seek Allah's help so he can make things easier for us.

I do not like doing hifz because I would have to do homework and study right after the class. However, Allah promised us that we will be rewarded if we read the Quran. I am good at reading and memorizing, and if I do not do Hifz, then I will be wasting my skills. Therefore, I should memorize the Quran even if I do not want to.

I also do not like cleaning the house, but if I do not clean the house, then it will become a mess. I won't be able to find my toys and play later. If I clean properly, then I can easily find my things, play, and be happy. I learned that if I do not try hard enough to fix the problem, then I am going to not like it even more. If I keep crying about not cleaning, then my problems won't disappear. It will grow even more! And that is why I should listen to my parents and clean.

One last thing that makes me feel upset is when my brother bothers me. Although it makes me mad, maybe he is bothering me because I did not listen to him, or he is trying to teach me something. I should be patient and not fight him.

The Prophet Muhammad (SAWS) used to get bothered by a lot of people, but he was always smiling and talking nicely to them. Similarly, I should also be nice to others even if they bother me. I should be positive and try to listen to them.

In surah Baqarah, ayah 216, Allah says:

"Battle has been enjoined upon you while it is hateful to you. But perhaps you hate a thing, and it is good for you; and perhaps you love a thing, and it is bad for you. And Allah knows, while you know not." [Al-Quran; 2:216]

This ayah tells me that there are times I don't like something that is good for me and there are times when I do like something that is bad for me. I should be patient during all times and remember that Allah will always make things easier for me if I am patient and kind.

There are things in life that I do not always like. I don't like to do Hifz, clean my room, and be bothered by my brother. However, as Muslims, we are taught to be patient when dealing with tests that annoy us and make us feel mad. I see that Allah knows and I don't know. So, I should listen to Allah, because he knows better than all of us.

3rd Place: Sulaiman O. Mansuri
Deen Home School, Champaign, IL

The troubles I face are very bothersome. I have mostly family problems. I get along more with my friends than with my family. My friends look out for me, respect me and play nicely with me. My brothers don't listen to me the same way that my friends do. My obstacles with my family make me feel frustrated, annoyed, and sad.

One of the issues that I have is with my baby brother. My baby brother is too small. He is three years old so, right now, I can't play rough with him. I feel frustrated that he is so small. When I need to stay positive, I try to remember that he will grow up one day, and then I can play with him however I would like. The Prophet (SAWS) said that

"He is not one of us who does not have mercy upon our young, respect our elders, and command good and forbid evil." [Sunan At-Tirmidhi]

This hadith really motivates me to be kind to my younger and older siblings because I want to be a part of the Prophet's (SAWS) ummah.

Another issue that I have in my family is with my older brother. My older brother doesn't take me seriously when I try to convince him to come outside and play sports with me. Whenever we are with my cousin, my cousin and my brother do not include me in their "club." They do not share with me when they have an opportunity to be kind. All of this makes me feel like I'm a ghost. But even though I'm sad, I feel a little bit better to know that the Prophet (SAWS) told us that if you are hurt but you are patient, then Allah (SWT) will forgive some of your sins.

"There is nothing (in the form of trouble) that comes to a believer even if it is the pricking of a thorn that there is decreed for him by Allah good or his sins are obliterated." [Sahih Muslim]

When I feel sad, I think of *"turning my sadness into kindness and turning my uniqueness into strength." [Naruto]* To me, this means that even if I'm sad, I can still be kind and respectful to other people. This also means I can turn what makes me special into power. Power to never give up.

Whenever I have problems with my family, I try to do this: I go outside, read the Quran, lay down, or wash my face. When I stay positive, I think about the good things, and remember the good advice people gave me. I take a deep breath and count to ten. Most importantly, I say

"Audhu billahi minashaitanir rajeem."

Young Muslim Voices

Special Recognition – Essay: Nabeeha Nur
Park International School and College, Dhaka

Our lives are very diverse. In this short life, we face many problems and gain knowledge on many different things. In our life, sometimes we become happy and sometimes we become sad because of many problems which harm us physically and mentally. Such a problem happened in my life which made me suffer emotionally and mentally. In this essay, I will highlight how I took the time of this problem positively and what role Islam has played. And what I have learned from the life of the Prophet of Islam (SAWS) is about having patience in bad situations.

It was about that time when I was in second grade. Then I had to leave my favorite school and move to another school because we had to change our home. Which gave me a lot of trouble mentally. It affected my mind also. Because the school where I used to go to, I had a lot of good friends in. And the education system was very good. Even the teachers were my favorite. So, in my new school, I used to miss my old friends, teachers, and school so much that I wasn't able to concentrate on my studies. It not only hampered my academic result and my concentration, but also my mental and physical health. Seeing my condition, my mother advised me something about patience from Qur'an and Hadith. How our Prophet (SAWS) used to keep patience when he faced problems in his life. And what Allah (SWT) says in Quran about keeping patience and having belief. In Hadith, the Prophet (SAWS) said,

"The real patience is at the first stroke of a calamity." [Sahih Al-Bukhari]

And in Holy Quran Allah (SWT) says,

"And seek help through patience and prayer; and indeed, it is difficult except for the humbly submissive [to Allah]" [Al-Quran; 2:45]

In this verse, the Quran reminds us that true patience is only for the humble, and for those who can understand that all joys and hardships are equally a blessing from Allah. So, I used to keep patient and keep praying to Allah (SWT) so that I would be able to pass the hard phase of my life. As in Quran Allah (SWT) says,

"So be patient with gracious patience." [Al-Quran; 70:5]

After some years, by the grace of almighty Allah, I came back to my previous school. Again, I got my old friends, old teachers and old environment. Alhamdulillah!

In conclusion, having belief and keeping patience got me this reward. What I have learned from Islam, from the Quran, and the Prophet (SAWS) is that we have to keep patience and belief in Allah whatever the situation is. I follow these rules, my mother's advice, and at the end of the day achieve what I wished. As Allah (SWT) says in Quran:

"Those will be awarded the Chamber (the most elevated portion of Paradise) for what they patiently endured, and they will be received therein with greetings and [words of] peace." [Al-Quran; 25:75]

**Special Recognition – Speech: Syeda Naffatul Jinan
Park International School and College, Dhaka**

Good times or bad times are obvious parts of our life. They come by turns like after winter comes spring. So, we have to accept both and deal with it. Although the second one is difficult. But I am inspired from the Holy Quran, life lessons of our Prophets, as well as my parents to face those difficulties with positivity. *"Sometimes Allah allows you to taste the bitterness of the world so you could fully appreciate the sweetness of faith"* –these words of Islamic scholar Omar Suleiman move me a lot to face the troubles that come to my life.

I have dealt with many problems in my life but the one I am going to describe now would be the biggest till date. A few months ago, my whole family needed to be hospitalized because of Dengue fever except me. I had to stay at my grandma's house for a few days and those few days were really tough for me. At that time, many people died because of Dengue in our country. I was so scared and shaken that I prayed to Allah (SWT) that my family could come back as soon as possible. I kept reciting the dua of Yunus (AS) all the time.

I know the story of Yunus (AS): when a huge fish swallowed him alive. Deep in the stomach of the whale, Yunus (AS) kept repeating *'La Ilaha Illa Anta Subhanaka inni Kuntu Minaz-Zalimin'*. Allah, the Most Merciful, was immensely moved by Yunus's (AS) repentance. He commanded the whale to spit out His messenger at the nearest shore. The whale obeyed Allah's command and our Prophet was saved from the stomach of the fish. I kept on being patient which is extremely helpful in any hard time as Allah has said,

"So do not weaken and do not grieve..." [Al-Quran; 3:139]

Our dear Prophet Hazrat Muhammad (SAWS) faced a lot of difficulties. We should follow his footsteps as he has laid down the perfect way of living life according to Allah's will. I was devastated when I heard my family's platelets were going down fast. I was at the edge of losing my courage. But I remembered the Hadith from Abu Hurairah (RA),

"He whom Allah intends good; He makes him to suffer from some affliction." [Sahih Al-Bukhari]

My mother and father's situation was going critical. I was overpowered by panic and could not imagine how I would survive in the world without my parents! Who will take care of me? My state of mind was beyond any explanation. But in my heart, I still had the ray of hope that Allah almighty is always there to listen to my prayer. I prayed and recited-

"For indeed, with hardship [will be] ease [i.e., relief]. Indeed, with hardship [will be] ease." [Al-Quran; 94:6]

I got the answer of my prayer when six days later when I saw my parents and younger sister were released from the hospital & came back home.

This difficulty of my life strengthened my belief and energy to face any adversity with a positive attitude. Now I can connect my experience with the difficult times of our great Prophet Muhammad (SAWS) and the hardships of other prophets. Their patience, their faith helped me dearly to pass that tough time I went through and the ones I am going to face in coming times with patience, aspirations and full faith in Almighty Allah. Now, I firmly believe that we get closer to Allah through difficulties.

MIDDLE SCHOOL | LEVEL 3

Topic:

The pre-teen years can be difficult as your mind and body are undergoing major changes and with all the constant peer pressure around you. How does Islam teach you to keep a sound mind with all the stressors you face on a daily basis? Outline a few methods you can use to maintain good mental health in your daily life.

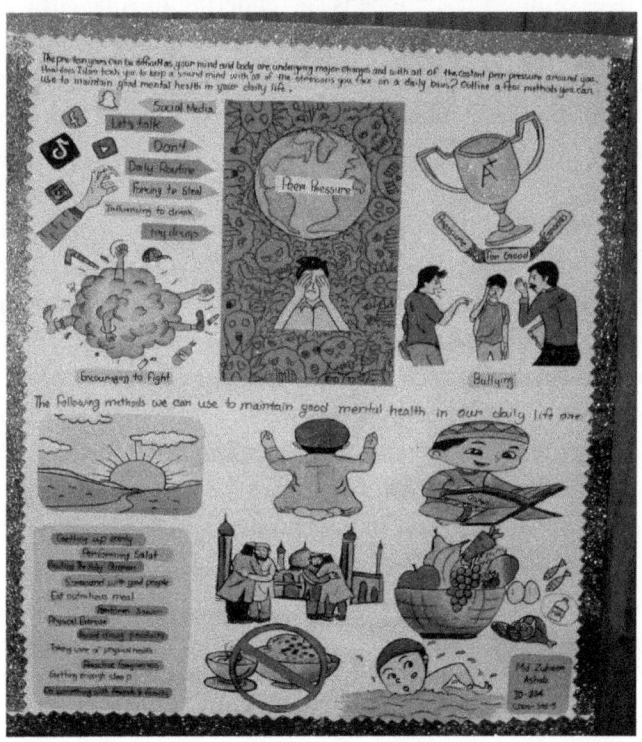

This poster was submitted by Zuhaer of level 3.

1st Place: Yusuf Mehmood
Homeschooling, Howard County, MD

Bzz! Bzz! My brain nerves are tingling with excitement. We have an urgent message to convey. Researchers have discovered the four lobes for a sound mind! Faith enters the heart, the heart communicates with the brain, and the brain commands the body to take planned action. The brain and the heart are in constant communication. They both play a crucial role in taking care of the body and maintaining mental health. The brain, being the powerhouse, controls the body and helps us overcome stress, anxiety, and panic. It is trained to mitigate risk, problem solve, and ensure peace of mind. The four lobes of the brain create a roadmap to overcome the dark challenges of life. The 1st lobe is surrendering to Allah. The 2nd is sharing and reflecting on our feelings. The 3rd lobe is creating a plan and devising a strategy. The 4th lobe is taking affirmative action. Let's zip through the neural pathways to discover the four lobes of the brain!

We have arrived at the first lobe of the brain. This lobe represents surrendering to Allah. As a Muslim, we must submit and surrender ourselves *entirely* to Allah. When hardship knocks on our door, our first instinct should be to make Dua (supplication) and increase our worship to Allah. Classical forms of this are sending durood upon the Prophet (SAWS), praying tahajjud, constant dhikr, heartfelt duas, and reading along with understanding the Quran. We must always remember that Allah has a plan for us even through trials and tribulations. Allah says in the Quran,

"Indeed, with hardship [will be] ease." [Al-Quran; 94:6]

Imagine leaning back into Allah's Hands for protection and comfort, He is the All-Powerful. This technique takes away the mental burden, providing safety and security.

Moving to the second lobe of the brain, sharing and reflecting on our feelings. A strategy for self-reflection is journaling. A good "brain dump" aids to get our problems out of our minds and onto a sheet of paper. Changing mediums, from thoughts to writing, helps to provide a different perspective to the problem. It is advisable that we share our feelings with mentors who have experience and wisdom. When choosing a mentor for guidance, search for someone who has attained inner peace and loves us. The goal is to find a solution, not to complain. Initially, we go inward with our struggle (journaling), then we go outward (sharing with others).

Zipping on to the third lobe of the brain. This lobe represents creating a plan and devising a strategy. There are various strategies that the brain can utilize. Making a list of pros and cons can be useful. This helps to categorize the issue. Another strategy is to figure out the worst- and best-case scenarios. This helps the brain to find a solution even when situations are tough. Another idea is to come up with multiple plans- plan A, plan B and plan C. When one fails, our brain can command our body to keep moving. Flexibility is the key to success. This is also a good time to listen to our hearts and our intuition. We are looking for joy, positivity and pleasing Allah in whatever we decide.

Finally, we have arrived at the fourth lobe of the brain. In this lobe, we must take affirmative action. This process depends on the individual situations and self-courage. The first and most difficult step is standing up for ourselves and addressing the situation. Facing the problem head on is the quickest way to solve it. Brushing it under the rug will only make it worse. There are times when having tried this step, we still come to a dead end. Then the best strategy is to remove ourselves from a harmful environment. Our environment plays a crucial role in our mindset, make sure it is positive! Prophet Muhammad (SAWS) was commanded to leave Makkah when the environment got too toxic. He was commanded to go to Madinah, where the helpers and friends were ready to aid the Muslims. Finally, we must have patience with Allah's plan. Allah says in the Quran,

"Peace be upon you for what you have patiently endured. And excellent is the final home." [Al-Quran; 13:24]

Insha' Allah in Jannah there will be no problems.

In conclusion, keeping a sound faith and a sound mind is the key to success. Positivity, joy and love will keep our Iman strong in our hearts. The four lobes of our brain method are a brilliant way for a sound mind. Surrendering to Allah, sharing and reflecting on our feelings, creating a plan and devising a strategy and taking affirmative action will ensure inner peace. This is a lifelong process, enjoy it!

2nd Place: Musa Rahmani
Al-Fatih Academy, Reston, VA

I'd like to begin by telling you all a story about an amazing experiment that Ibn Sina, a famous scholar, once did. Ibn Sina placed two identical sheep in cages, side by side. Then, he placed a wolf in a cage and put the cage near the sheep, but only so that one of them could see the wolf. Soon, the sheep near the wolf died but the other who could not see the wolf was healthy. Subhanallah! Even though the sheep could only see the wolf, the unnecessary stress and fear that this had caused affected him so much. Ibn Sina's experiment is an amazing lesson about what can happen to our mental and physical health because of the stressors that we all face in our daily lives. And, you know what? There's so much to stress out about nowadays! School, work, family, tests, and to add to all of that – adjusting to a "new normal" because of COVID. If we do not manage these stressors and maintain good mental health, we too will suffer. Today, I'd like to talk about three methods that we can all use to maintain good mental health.

The first and most important method is to strengthen our spiritual condition. As Muslims, during every trial we face, we should return to what is most important to us – our Emaan. So, what do our most important sources say about dealing with all our struggles? In Surah Ash-Sharh, verses 5-6 of the Quran, Allah (SWT) says:

"For indeed, with hardship [will be] ease [i.e., relief]. Indeed, with hardship [will be] ease." [Al-Quran; 94:5- 6]

In Surah Al-Baqarah, verse 45, He says,

"And seek help through patience and prayer; and indeed, it is difficult except for the humbly submissive [to Allah]" [Al-Quran; 2:45]

So, this means that instead of having a "doom and gloom" mentality when we face troubles, we should remember that both hardship and ease comes from Allah (SWT) and that He will show us the way through trials. Another important lesson comes from the Prophet (SAWS) when he told us,

"He whom Allah intends good; He makes him to suffer from some affliction." [Sahih Al-Bukhari]

Instead of thinking that mental health problems are a sign that we are being punished, we must remember that Allah (SWT) loves us and wants us to come out of our troubles as stronger Muslims. Prophet Yaqoub (AS) waited for years to see Prophet Yusuf again and was in deep sorrow but remained patient and faithful because he knew this was a test from Allah (SWT). So, the first method is to always return to our Creator during times of struggle.

The second method is to take time away from stressful environments and have healthy outlets to take our mind off our stressors. When we feel stressed, it's important to get off our screens, have some quiet time to ourselves, and do something productive that's good for us, like exercising. The Prophet Muhammad (SAWS) taught us to maintain our emotions and would give lessons such as,

"When one of you becomes angry while standing, he should sit down. If the anger leaves him, well and good; otherwise, he should lie down." [Sunan Abi Dawud]

In addition, the Prophet (SAWS) lived a life of moderation and taught us the importance of healthy eating and sleeping in moderation. He would fast often and spend some of the night sleeping and the rest praying. He would tell his companions,

"...Your body has a right over you..." [Sahih Al-Bukhari]

So, the second method is to maintain our emotions and take care of both our physical and mental health by doing Thikr, reading the Quran, eating healthy foods, exercising, and sleeping well.

The final method is to surround ourselves with positivity and positive people. If we allow our surroundings to cause us unnecessary anxiety and stress, our health will suffer. Focusing on the positive aspects of life and remembering all the countless blessings that Allah (SWT) has given us will remind us to be grateful during all conditions. It is also important that we have positive people in our life who will support us. We should seek help from those who are close to us to lend us an ear and listen to our troubles. By following these three methods, we will be able to maintain good mental health, inshallah! Above all, it is important to remember the words of our Prophet (SAWS) who told us,

"Allah is sufficient for us, and He is an excellent guardian, and we repose our trust in Allah."

Young Muslim Voices

3rd Place: Hamza-Syed Ali
Homeschooling, Gaithersburg, MD

As a Muslim, I know that the reason I was created is to worship Allah (SWT). I also know everything that happens in my life is a test from Allah (SWT). This includes mental health issues. One challenge to maintaining mental health is knowing when you have problems. It is easier to identify physical health issues because you can usually see it. Mental health problems are hard to explain since we cannot see feelings. Many times, we focus on physical health and ignore mental health. Muslims are responsible for taking care of blessings Allah (SWT) has provided including physical and mental health. Allah (SWT) says:

"...and do not throw [yourselves] with your [own] hands into destruction..." [Al-Quran; 2:195]

Failing to take care of physical and mental health means you are harming yourself. I will talk about some ways for us to deal with mental health issues.

The first way to maintain good mental health is to stay in touch with the Quran. This means we should read, listen, and think about the meaning of the Quran every day. Allah's (SWT) words remind us why we are on Earth – to worship Allah. The Quran is the first shifa. Allah (SWT) says,

"And We send down of the Qurʾān that which is healing and mercy for the believers, but it does not increase the wrongdoers except in loss." [Al-Quran; 17:82]

When facing mental health challenges, turning to the Quran will provide comfort.

The next way is to call out to Allah when we are not feeling happy. We should make dua to Allah (SWT) to help us. Allah says:

"Those who have believed and whose hearts are assured by the remembrance of Allah. Unquestionably, by the remembrance of Allah hearts are assured." [Al-Quran; 13:28]

It is very clear when we call out to Allah (SWT), He always hears and helps. We should remember when we make Dua to Allah (SWT), He answers all of our Duas.

The third way to deal with mental health issues is to not think too much about the past or the future. We need to live in the present. If we make mistakes, we need to ask Allah's forgiveness and know we are forgiven. We should not spend too much time thinking about the future since that is something Allah controls. Instead, we should focus on all the blessings Allah (SWT) has given in the present time and be grateful for them.

The fourth way is to spend time with our family and others. While it is harder to spend time outside of our homes during COVID-19, we should use the time we have with our family. Anas (RA) narrates RasulAllah (SAWS) said,

"Whoever loves that he be granted more wealth and that his lease of life be prolonged then he should keep good relations with his Kith and kin." [Sahih Al-Bukhari]

When we spend time with our families, we often cannot remember our mental health issues. They can even provide suggestions for dealing with stress or other mental health issues.

The next way to maintain mental health is being physically active. This one seems less obvious, increasing physical activity improves mental health. Abu Hurairah (RA) narrates, RasulAllah (SAWS) said:

"A strong believer is better and is more lovable to Allah than a weak believer, and there is good in everyone..." [Sahih Muslim]

This hadith shows Muslims need to work on being healthy. People are less willing to be physically active these days. We should spend less time online and more time on physical activity to improve our health.

The final thing we can do is talk to our parents and seek professional medical help for mental health issues. Our parents cannot help if they do not know that we have mental health issues. When needed, our parents can help us get professional help from a mental health doctor. We use doctors for physical health, so why not mental health? Anas (RA) narrates RasulAllah (SAWS) said:

"There is no disease that Allah has created, except that He also has created its treatment." [Sahih Al-Bukhari]

Just as Allah (SWT) created cures for physical health issues, Allah (SWT) also created cures for mental health issues.

Alhamdulilah, researching mental health, I realized that it is as important as physical health. I discussed several things we can do to maintain our mental health. We begin by staying in touch with the Quran and making Dua to Allah (SWT). We need to be thankful for all the blessings Allah (SWT) has given us in the present time. We should spend time with our families since this will help us reduce stress. We should work on being physically active because it improves mental health. Finally, we need to speak with our parents, so they get us medical help when we need it.

Special Recognition – Essay: Dawud Mansuri
Deen Home School, Champaign, IL

First and foremost, as a ten-year-old boy, I don't think I am currently undergoing many changes in my body. I am still very young and have not matured yet. As a homeschooled student, I am also not touched by much peer pressure or major stressors. Nonetheless, I still believe mental health is one of the most important things in our life. To have good mental health you have to have three things: good physical health, good spirituality and good use of your free time. There is a hadith narrated by Ibn Abbas, Muhammad (SAWS) said,

"There are two blessings many people are deceived into losing: health and free time." [Sahih Al-Bukhari]

Our physical health is very important because if we have bad physical health this may lead to bad mental health and make us distracted from our goal. Allah has forbidden us from drinking wine, smoking, and eating pig. The physical benefit of listening to what Allah has forbidden us from is that we are safeguarding our body from diseases and other illnesses. Muhammad (SAWS) used to do things like archery, horseback riding, and swimming. He would stay active and in good shape. That means that we should try to follow his actions and be energetic just like him.

A good and pure spiritual heart is one of the keys to excellent mental health. To have a good heart, you have to have good manners and character. You also have to pray and make your heart clean by not doing bad deeds. If you fall short, you should perform a good deed to wipe the bad deed away. Keeping your heart clean is hard sometimes. Once in a while, you should perform tawbah and seek the forgiveness of Allah, and the forgiveness of the person you have wronged.

There is a saying that, *"An idle mind is a devil's workshop, and idle hands are a devil's tools."* This means if we are indolent and we use our free time being slothful, then we will be like servants for Shaitan. Wasting time is a very easy sin to commit; watching too much TV, playing too many video games, and getting caught up on social media for a long time, are all things we should avoid. If we don't do good things for our bodies and souls, then we will end up wasting the time that Allah (SWT) has granted us on this beautiful earth.

To conclude,

"There is hope, even when your brain tells you there isn't." [John Green]

Thankfully, Islam shows us that there is hope. Islam teaches us that to have good mental health, you must work on physical health, spirituality, and good use of free time. By the grace of Allah, we have in the Quran and the Hadith, the best examples of how to have good mental health.

Special Recognition – Speech: Sakina Mansuri
Deen Home School, Champaign, IL

"When it is darkest, we can see the stars." – Ralph Waldo Emerson

When I am in the dark, the pieces of Islam are my stars. As a tween, some of the struggles I face are knowing and understanding who I am, coming to terms with feeling like the odd one out, and worrying about what others think about me. Islam helps me to keep a sound mind by giving me: hijab as a protection, Muhammad (SAWS) as my role model, and the freedom to focus on pleasing only Allah. Islam teaches me to always remember Allah if I need help, and Allah helps me with anything and everything I need.

To begin with, knowing and understanding who I am is troublesome for me because there are so many things that make me, me. I love playing sports, watching anime, and listening to music on long car rides. I also enjoy reading, writing short stories, and doing arts and crafts. With all the different things that are part of me, it is hard for me to know which part identifies me. But then, every morning when I put my hijab on, I conclude that Islam is the biggest and most important feature of my identity. If I let other parts of me take over instead of the Islamic part, music and anime would take over my mind and life immediately. Hijab is my shield, it is my protection from my nafs, not just a piece of cloth wrapped on top of my head.

Even though I go to a Muslim Co-op, I still feel like I stick out from the rest of my classmates. I try to dress modestly, but this is challenging because the people around me and on social media dress differently. When I talk, I feel like my speech is different from all my friends' speech. I don't curse, I don't make fun of people, and I don't complain about my teachers. I try to be the one who does the right thing, and it's challenging because sometimes it feels like I am the only one thinking about it. The Qur'an gives me a solution,

"There has certainly been for you in the Messenger of Allah an excellent pattern (an example to be followed) ..." [Al-Quran; 33:21]

When I read this ayah, I remember how the Prophet (SAWS) also stuck out when he first started preaching Islam. His message was not popular, but he was patient with it for Allah's sake. I feel like I am not alone. I remind myself that sticking out will all be worth it one day.

Not worrying what other people think about me is one of my struggles. I am constantly worried about what I am doing and how others might react to it. Sometimes, I find myself acting differently when I am in different spaces. I try to go for that cool/tough girl personality. But while being tough might look cool, it makes me seem careless. When it comes to academics, for example, it might look like I don't care, when I really love to learn. One of the things that help me forget about impressing other people is realizing that Islam is freeing us. We don't have to worry about impressing other people, just Allah! For example, if you go out of your way to do something for someone, and they don't acknowledge you for it, you will feel disappointed, but when you do something for Allah, He will remember– no matter what.

"Indeed, with hardship [will be] ease." [Al-Quran; 94:6]

In the Quran, Allah promises ease after hardship. Even though I am affected by these obstacles– my identity, sticking out, and being insouciant about what others think—Islam gives me solutions. I remind myself every time I fall and feel like giving up, that if I can last a little longer, I will have peace.

MIDDLE SCHOOL | LEVEL 4

Topic:

The pre-teen years can be difficult as your mind and body are undergoing major changes and with all the constant peer pressure around you. How does Islam teach you to keep a sound mind with all the stressors you face on a daily basis? Outline a few methods you can use to maintain good mental health in your daily life.

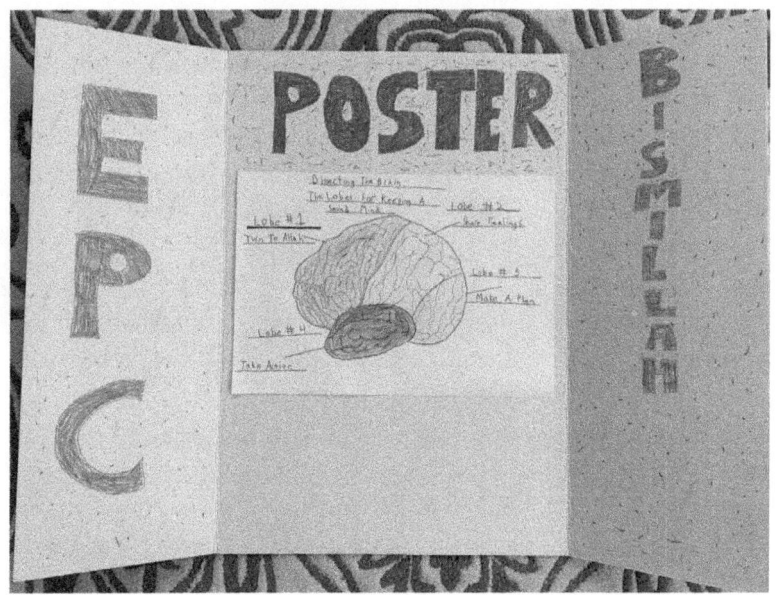

This poster was submitted by Yusuf Mehmood of level 3.

1st Place: Mariyah Mehmood
Homeschooling, Howard County, MD

"Lub, dub! Lub, dub!" echoes the beating of my heart. This is the most magical organ of my body; every beat allows me to survive! Prophet Muhammad (SAWS) said,

"There is a piece of flesh in the body if it becomes good (reformed) the whole body becomes good but if it gets spoilt the whole body gets spoilt and that is the heart." [Sahih Al-Bukhari]

This hadith is evidence that the heart is connected to the mind, in order for a sound mind you need a sound heart. Allah puts Iman (faith) into your heart, your heart communicates with your mind and your mind controls your body systems. There are four chambers in the spiritual heart designed to help overcome life's curveballs. The first chamber is turning to Allah in the face of adversity. The second chamber is sharing your feelings. The third chamber is strategizing and discovering solutions. The last chamber is taking action and moving towards a resolution. For this process to be efficient, you must have a tight rope connection up to Allah.

The first chamber of the spiritual heart is turning to Allah in the face of adversity. Always remember that Allah has a large-scale view and opens doors accordingly. When adversity comes your way, analyze your body's response. Train yourself to turn to Allah immediately. In the Quran, Allah says

"Unquestionably, by the remembrance of Allah hearts are assured." [Al-Quran; 13:28]

Constant dhikr (remembrances), praying tahajjud, reciting Quran will fill your heart with inner peace and comfort. Igniting your heart with the flame of Iman (faith) will light up your journey of life. This vital step will affirm your faith and maintain a sound mind.

The second chamber of the heart is sharing your feelings. Initially, journaling can be a useful tool for self-reflection. Gifting yourself the grace and space to express your feelings in a safe space is the ultimate form of self-love. After going inwards, consider sharing your well-constructed thoughts with trusted mentors. Your mentor should embody wisdom, inner peace, love, trustworthiness and experience. Sharing is a beautiful strategy for human connection and obtaining multiple perspectives.

Next, the third chamber is strategizing and discovering solutions. Listen to your heart's desires and focus with a solution-oriented mindset. You can create a list, write out a 'pros and cons' list or create 'worst case and best case' scenario plans. Multiple options present your mind with flexibility. The fear of feeling trapped is when sadness, grief and depression take root. These dark feelings can quickly grow and ultimately destroy your mental health.

Lastly, the fourth chamber is to take action. Depending on the problem, you may want to stand up for yourself with confidence. Other times you will realize the wise decision is to distance yourself. Your environment influences you and plays a crucial role in your mental health. There is a hadith where the Prophet (SAWS) said

"The example of a good companion (who sits with you) in comparison with a bad one, is like that of the musk seller and the blacksmith's bellows (or furnace); from the first you would either buy musk or enjoy its good smell while the bellows would either burn your clothes or your house, or you get a bad nasty smell thereof." [Sahih Al-Bukhari]

Surround yourself with believers who have the same goal- seeking the pleasure of Allah.

In conclusion, I pray that these four chambers for a sound heart resonate with you. When blessings appear scarce, turn to Allah for abundance and light. Align your heart, mind and body to seek the pleasure of Allah. All your problems will fall away, you will begin to view the world with a positive and bright outlook. The four chambers method of turning to Allah, sharing your feelings, discovering solutions and taking action can solve any problem. My ambition is to be immersed in SibghatulAllah (Color of Allah) with peace, light and love.

2nd Place: Hafsah Khan
Clarksville Elementary School, Clarksville, MD

Tiktok, new shoes, music, Instagram, school violence, math tests, middle school, making new friends, masking, procrastinating, Covid rules, what's next? As a 7th grader going to public school, the pressures around me make me feel like a balloon about to explode! Alhamdullilah, I am a Muslim which helps to release the pressure from that balloon. Islam teaches us many strategies to deal with the pressures and stresses that surround us.

One way that we can deal with the stresses around us is to talk to an adult or friend. After the Prophet (SAWS) met angel Gibrail for the first time, he was very scared and ran to Khadijah (RA) and told her to cover him. After he told Khadijah (RA) what had happened, she comforted him and then took him to visit her very wise cousin, Waraqa. Her cousin told them that Muhammad (SAWS) meeting angel Gibrail was a sign of him becoming a prophet. Just as the Prophet (SAWS) did, we can talk to someone to relieve the pressures we feel when we are scared and overwhelmed. We can talk to our parents, trusted adults, teachers, or counselors so that they can help us to figure out solutions to our stressors and give us words of comfort.

Another strategy that can help prevent the pressures around us is to have good friends that respect our values. "Did you watch the new music video?", "Let's do a Tiktok dance!" These are some of the peer pressures a middle schooler faces on a regular basis. Having to choose between being accepted by our friends and doing what is pleasing to Allah (SWT) can create unnecessary pressure. Prophet Muhammad (SAWS) said:

"The example of a good companion (who sits with you) in comparison with a bad one, is like that of the musk seller and the blacksmith's

bellows (or furnace); from the first you would either buy musk or enjoy its good smell while the bellows would either burn your clothes or your house, or you get a bad nasty smell thereof." [Sahih Al-Bukhari]

According to this hadith, if we hang out with someone with good manners and character, their good traits will rub off on us and if we hang out with someone whose actions are not pleasing to Allah (SWT), their bad habits could rub off on us.

Lastly and most importantly, we must ask Allah (SWT) for help when feeling stressed or overwhelmed. In surah Ale Imran, ayah 173, Allah (SWT) says,

"Those to whom people [i.e., hypocrites] said, "Indeed, the people have gathered against you, so fear them." But it [merely] increased them in faith, and they said, "Sufficient for us is Allah, and [He is] the best Disposer of affairs."" [Al-Quran; 3:173]

In the battle of Uhud, the disbelievers came to the Muslims and wanted them scared by saying more men are coming against them. The Muslims became stronger and replied with *"Sufficient for us is Allah, and [He is] the best Disposer of affairs.""* [Al-Quran; 3:173]

Even though the Muslims lost the battle of Uhud, they had strong belief in Allah (SWT) and His plan. He knows what we can handle and has promised us,

"Indeed, with hardship [will be] ease." [Al-Quran; 94:6]

When we are feeling overwhelmed, we should be comforted by these words because Allah (SWT) is our creator and knows us best.

Islam teaches us many strategies to deal with the difficulties and stresses that surround us. If we are ever feeling stressed, we should talk to an adult so that they can comfort us and talk us through solutions to our problems. We should also choose our friends wisely so that they don't encourage us to do what is displeasing to Allah (SWT). The most important strategy that we should never forget is to ask Allah (SWT) for help through duas that we have been taught. Insha Allah, I pray that by using these strategies, I am able to keep afloat with my balloon and fly high with Eman.

3rd Place: Sakinah Ozair
Al-Tibyaan, Bayaan Academy, Baltimore, MD

Every year, 1 out of 6 young people ranging from the ages of 6 to 17 are struck with a mental health disorder, according to the National Alliance on Mental Illness. Mental health issues in youth are widespread, potentially due to peer pressure, stress, and physical and emotional changes. Because strong mental health is crucial, the proper tools are needed to take care of the mind. Using the teachings of Islam, mental health can be improved using physical, emotional, and spiritual tools that bring you closer to Allah (SWT).

Islam proves to us that spending time outside and getting fresh air and enough sleep can improve mental health. To start off, spending time outside and getting fresh air is a great way to boost your mood and have a positive mindset. When you're surrounded with Allah's (SWT) creations, you feel closer to Him. In addition, getting enough sleep can help. When you get the amount of sleep needed, you will not only feel happier but also more alert and focused throughout the day. This can help with daily activities such as school and ibaadah. In Surah Rum, ayah 23, Allah (SWT) says:

"And of His signs is your sleep by night and day and your seeking of His bounty. Indeed, in that are signs for a people who listen." [Al-Quran; 30:23]

This ayah states that the night is for sleep, which we should follow, which can improve mental health.

Emotional tools also come from teachings of Islam. For example, mindfulness helps you feel more grateful and satisfied with the blessings of Allah. In Surah Naml, ayah 73, Allah (SWT) states:

"And indeed, your Lord is the possessor of bounty for the people, but most of them are not grateful." [Al-Quran; 27:73]

Being grateful is crucial when it comes to improving well-being. In addition, avoiding negative thoughts can make you happier and focus on positive subjects more. Furthermore, by talking about your feelings to someone you trust, you can improve your mental health. You can feel less anxious and stressed talking with somebody such as a family member. When you stay connected with family, you feel happier and less lonely. Not only do you feel more pleased, but you also follow the teachings of Prophet Muhammad (SAWS). In Sunan Ibn Majah, Hadith 4212 states that it was narrated from 'Aishah, the mother of the Believers, that the Prophet (SAWS) said:

"The most quickly rewarded of good deeds are kindness and upholding the ties of kinship, and the most quickly punished evil deeds are injustice and severing the ties of kinship." [Sunan Ibn Majah]

This hadith shows us that staying connected with family is extremely important and beneficial.

What spiritual tools does Islam teach us to use in order to maintain good mental health? Along with salah, adhkar, and reading the Quran, there are other ways to improve mental health spiritually. One example is by forgiving others. When you forgive someone, you remember Allah (SWT) more, which can help ease stress and anxiety you might have, knowing that Allah (SWT) has control over everything. Forgiving another person can help you have less stress, anxiety, and depression symptoms. Another tool that can help mental health is dua and having trust in Allah (SWT). When you make dua, you can ask for anything, knowing that Allah is with you, and He is the best of planners. In Surah Baqarah, ayah 186, Allah (SWT) says:

"And when My servants ask you, [O Muḥammad], concerning Me - indeed I am near. I respond to the invocation of the supplicant when he calls upon Me. So let them respond to Me [by obedience] and believe in Me that they may be [rightly] guided." [Al-Quran; 2:186]

Youngsters go through many physical and emotional changes along with stress and peer pressure. Mental health can be impacted in many ways and to keep your mind and soul healthy, the right tools are needed. Using physical, emotional, and spiritual tools from the teachings of Islam that bring you closer to Allah (SWT), mental health can be improved. These tools and gaining a closer relationship with Allah (SWT) can help keep your mind and body sound.

Special Recognition – Essay: Iffat Chowdhury
Al-Huda School, College Park, MD

I still remember the day when I first landed in the United States. It wasn't easy to leave my mom and come to a whole different country alone with my dad. It wasn't easy leaving my childhood friends, my home, and relatives at the age of 13. It wasn't easy adapting to American middle school life while speaking a different language. It certainly has not been easy to learn and make friends during the middle of a pandemic. Having online classes has made it even harder for me to interact with others and learn the language properly. Making a friend is not easy but it is even harder when we are in a pandemic, having fewer social interactions, and not being able to speak the language properly. There are many other problems that I am facing right now but the main reason why I am feeling down and depressed is that I can't share my problems with anyone, and I don't have anyone to connect with. If the bad things continue, then it will create more problems and many other outcomes can arise from these problems such as, 1. Being unhappy 2. Jealous 3. Angry. Islam can help us in many ways to tackle these problems.

During this winter break, I went on a trip with my family. However, even with my family, I felt that I was alone, and didn't have anyone close to my age so I felt left out. I was constantly wishing I could go back to my hometown and spend time with my friends there. But then I realized that even if I go back to Bangladesh, my life won't be the same. I would still have to go to a new school and face many other problems there. If I keep blaming my situations, my problems won't disappear. Instead of being unhappy about my circumstances which I can't control right now, I should focus on staying positive and making the most out of my current state. Many people in my country are desperately wanting to come here for a better life. I should be grateful that I was able to come to a country where there's many other opportunities available for me. As Allah says in the Quran,

"Indeed, with hardship [will be] ease." [Al-Quran; 94:6]

This ayah is a reminder that we all face difficulties in our life. But nothing good can be achieved if we don't go through hardships. If we stay calm, patient, and have faith in Allah, insha-Allah we will be able to overcome any difficult situations. Being emotional, pessimistic, or holding a negative attitude towards someone will only lead to an unpleasant impact, it will affect our mental health negatively, and prevent us from being happy.

Anxiety is a test from Allah. Even the prophets during their lives have gone through many difficult situations. However, they didn't give up, they were hopeful, and Allah certainly had made things easier for them. As a reminder, I should be thankful that I am attending a Muslim school in America, receiving a better education than before. Many people don't have the opportunity to do that. I am blessed that I am surrounded by Muslims even in my school and learning so much about my religion which will only take me closer to my deen and Allah. If I stayed back in my country, this wouldn't have been possible. Likewise, it is better to have one or two close friends who can help me get closer to Allah, prepare me for the hereafter than having multiple friends who can negatively influence my behavior, leading me to a negative path. Surely, my life has changed here, and I have many difficulties. However, there is no guarantee that my life will be easier if I go back to my hometown and avoid my problems. As Allah says in Surah Duha, ayah 1-3,

"By the morning brightness; And [by] the night when it covers with darkness, Your Lord has not taken leave of you, [O Muhammad], nor has He detested [you]." [Al-Quran; 93:1-3]

Just like the dark nights that pass every day with a beautiful sunrise, our lives can also take some turns and become dark. Nonetheless, it doesn't mean that we won't see the light. We should be hopeful and have faith in Allah's words.

During those dark times of our lives, we should keep trying and insha-Allah, we will be able to find the bright side of our life as well. This surah gives us hope and teaches us that Allah will never abandon us, he knows about our problems, and knows that we are trying our best.

If we don't learn how to control ourselves during rough times, and keep blaming our situations, we will never be able to see the bright sides of our life, never find happiness, and our mental health can only decline. If we take some time to read the stories of our Prophets and his companions, we will learn that they have gone through much more difficult scenarios than what most of us are currently tackling. However, they have all succeeded in their lives because they had faith in Allah. The verses of the Quran can provide us with hope which can help us not fall into despair and motivate us to become more optimistic. Thus, we too can overcome our difficulties and improve our mental health.

Special Recognition – Speech: Tasneem -Syeda Ali
Homeschooling, Gaithersburg, VA

According to the CDC, mental health includes our emotional, psychological, and social well-being. Mental health issues are evidence of faith not evidence against it. This misconception that mental health issues are not a part of Islam, is backward and simply wrong. Mental health problems are a part of human nature, as Allah (SWT) says:

"Indeed, mankind was created anxious." [Al-Quran; 70:19]

The most righteous of people, the Prophets, faced challenges to their mental health. Sadly we, the Muslim community, continue to downplay mental health problems, which is why American Muslims are two times more likely to have attempted suicide compared with other religious groups, according to JAMA Psychiatry. We must explore methods to maintain our mental health.

The first way to preserve our mental health is to call out to the Almighty. As Allah (SWT) says:

"O you who have believed, seek help through patience and prayer. Indeed, Allah is with the patient." [Surah Al- Baqarah; 2:153]

We are told to call out to the one in control. Ask Him for anything, indeed He can make the impossible possible. Furthermore, connecting with Allah means having a connection with His book, the greatest miracle, and a cure for all things, as Allah (SWT) says in the Qur'an:

"And We send down of the Quran that which is healing and mercy for the believers" [Al-Quran; 17:82]

Keep the Qur'an close to your heart. Read, recite, understand, and apply it. Having a connection to Allah and His book are the main ways to maintain our mental health, however, it does not end there. Anas (RA) reported:

A man said, "O Messenger of Allah, should I tie my camel and trust in Allah, or should I leave her untied and trust in Allah?" The Prophet, peace and blessings be upon him, said, "Tie her and trust in Allah." [Sunan At-Tirmidhi]

We must 'tie our camel' in everything. We must do our part. Having Tawakkul and doing our part are simultaneous. When we deal with these issues, we must 'tie our camel' by seeking expert help. Unfortunately, many Muslims refuse, because they fall prey to the backward misconception, that these issues are not a part of Islam and something to be ashamed of.

There are some practical things we can do to help our mental health. Keeping ourselves socially active is vital in preserving our mental health. Humans are social beings. Yes, COVID-19 has made this task difficult. However, Allah gave us alternatives to the situation - like meeting with people online. If we cannot for some reason go outside or meet online, we engage with our families. We cannot lock ourselves in our bubbles because that will lead to a lack of social involvement and potential mental health problems. However, in being socially active, we must pay attention to who we choose as our close companions. AbuMusa (RA) narrates, RasulAllah (SAWS) said:

"The example of a good companion (who sits with you) in comparison with a bad one, is like that of the musk seller and the blacksmith's bellows (or furnace); from the first you would either buy musk or enjoy its good smell while the bellows would either burn your clothes or your house, or you get a bad nasty smell thereof." [Sahih al-Bukhari]

According to WebMD, a bad friend can be many things, but, typically, they lead to mental and emotional fatigue or a lack of general well-being.

Moreover, we must guard our physical health because that influences our mental health. If we have a physical health problem, we are highly likely to have a mental health problem, according to the Mental Health Foundation. In Islam, we are taught to take of ourselves. Ibn Amr (RA) narrates, RasulAllah (SAWS) said:

"...Your body has a right over you..." [Sahih Al-Bukhari]

We should eat healthy and exercise. Research shows that exercising can reduce anxiety and depression, according to the NIH.

In conclusion, Alhamdulillah, I outlined a few methods that can help us live a healthy life, insha'Allah. During this pandemic, there has been a sharp rise in mental health issues, because humans are social beings, one of the main causes of these issues is lack of social involvement. We must have Tawakkul and concurrently 'tie our camel.' Having Tawakkul, by praying and keeping the Qur'an with us. Taking further action, by speaking to experts, keeping ourselves socially involved, choosing our companions well, and keeping ourselves physically healthy. If we can do these things, we can live a healthy life, insha'Allah. Finally, we must let go of this backward stigma, that mental health issues are not a part of Islam. I end with one question, will we not sound the alarm, when countless lives have been lost and continue to be lost because of these issues?

HIGH SCHOOL | LEVEL 6

Topic:

There are many challenges in the teen and adolescent years that high schoolers face daily. As a Muslim, how can you navigate all these challenges while staying positive and mentally healthy? Discuss what adults in your life and your community can do to help young people handle stress.

Young Muslim Voices

1st Place: Khadijja Bah
Al-Huda School, College Park, MD

Having straight A's, getting an internship, and acing my SATs are just a few of the things that plague my mind as an 11th grader. It's almost the end of my high school career, and I'm overwhelmed with feelings of unfulfillment, self-disappointment, anxiety, and stress. It seems that I have so many things that I need to accomplish, but time is running out and fast. Many teens feel the same way, Muslim and non-Muslim alike. The difference between the two groups is that Muslims have a solution for the challenges we face as teens and adolescence. It's just up to us, our families, and the community to apply them.

There is an epidemic plaguing society, an increase of depression among teens in America. According to the National Survey on Drug Use and Health, depression in youth aged 12-17 increased by at least 4.9% over 12 years. According to Pew Research, 70% of American teens agree that anxiety and depression are significant concerns among their peers. What this data shows is very concerning.

As Muslims, we recognize that feelings of anxiety, laziness, and stress are attributable to diseases of the heart. The heart is the king of the body. The Prophet said,

'There is a piece of flesh in the body if it becomes good (reformed) the whole body becomes good but if it gets spoilt the whole body gets spoilt and that is the heart." [Sahih al-Bukhari]

The first step in purifying oneself is acknowledging our purpose on Earth. Allah says in the Quran,

"And I did not create the jinn and mankind except to worship Me." [Al-Quran; 51:56]

This ayah clearly shows us that worshiping Allah alone is the purpose of our creation. If we do not worship Allah, then we will feel unfulfilled. Worshiping Allah consists of and is not limited to praying the five daily salah, fasting, and giving zakat. Doing these actions will help to purify the heart and remove the disease. This will, in turn, remove the anxiety and stress from us.

One of the downfalls of Muslims is that we don't recognize how much mental health is stressed in the Quran and Sunnah. Surah Duha is deemed by many to be the cure to all ailments involving mental health. Allah tells us in the Surah,

"Your Lord has not taken leave of you, [O Muhammad], nor has He detested [you]... And your Lord is going to give you, and you will be satisfied." [Al-Quran; 93:3-5]

These ayahs clearly show that Allah will always be there for us in hardship and ease. Surah Duha was revealed during a rough period of the Prophet's life. Allah revealed this Surah to aid the Prophet. Allah also says in the Quran,

"Do not grieve; indeed, Allah is with us." [Al-Quran; 9:40]

Parents and community members can aid Muslim teens by remembering that this life is not the end goal. Our goal is to enter Jannah. Yes, as Muslims we should always strive for excellence in everything that we do, but we shouldn't overexert ourselves. Abu 'Ubaydah reported: Mutarrif Ibn Abdullah, may Allah have mercy on him, said,

"The best of matters is the middle course, for a good deed is between two evil deeds." [Tarikh Dimashq]

In Islam, everything has a right over us even our bodies and our health. Parents just need to remember that teens are humans, and we're not perfect. We're not robots and we need breaks to recharge.

Islam is not just a religion, but a way of life. It has solutions for many things even for the challenges that teens face today. All that needs to be done is for the solutions to be applied. Not just by the teens themselves, but by the Muslim community as a whole.

2nd Place: Emira Syeda Ali
Homeschooling, Gaithersburg, VA

The challenges faced by young adults are tests from Allah (SWT). Allah (SWT) says in the Quran:

"And We will surely test you with something of fear and hunger and a loss of wealth and lives and fruits but give good tidings to the patient." [Al-Quran; 2:155]

A common misconception among the Ummah, about mental problems, is someone with mental health issues either has weak faith or does not have enough trust in Allah (SWT). Abu-Zayd Al-Balkhi challenged this notion. He argued,

"Humans are composed of a body and a psyche, and that we can face health and sickness in both. The same way our bodies experience fever, headaches, and pain, our minds can experience psychological symptoms such as anger, sorrow, fear, and panic."

Al-Balkhi recognized that mental illness was an affliction that needed to be treated, not a sin to be met with punishment or shame.

The prevalence of mental illness among Muslims is high. According to JAMA Physiatry: American Muslims are twice as likely to attempt suicide than any other group. Researchers attribute the high suicide attempt rate to two factors: religious discrimination and community stigma — both of which, they say, prevent Muslim American communities from seeking mental health services. COVID-19 has increased the level of mental health issues. According to the CDC,

"Public health actions are necessary to reduce the spread of COVID-19, but they can make us feel isolated and lonely and can increase stress and anxiety."

All of this shows how serious mental health issues among the Muslim community have gotten. Despite this, the stigma remains. Therefore, we must address how Muslims should maintain their mental health.

There is no way to prevent mental health issues as those are tests from Allah (SWT), but there are things we can do to ease it. The primary step is simple – rely on the Quran. We need to read, listen, understand, and apply its lessons to our lives. Just by doing these things we will realize the purpose of life and maintain a healthy attitude. As Allah (SWT) says in the Quran:

"And We send down of the Qurān that which is healing and mercy for the believers, but it does not increase the wrongdoers except in loss." [Al-Quran; 17:82]

Remarkably, in 2019, the NIH did a study on how to reduce depression. One group listened to the Quran, while another listened to relaxing music. After four weeks, results show the group who listened to the Quran had a greater decrease in depression than those who listened to music. SubhanAllah! With Allah's permission, just listening to the Quran can reduce depression.

The next step that one needs to take to stay positive and maintain a healthy attitude is to make Dua. Dua is crucial in our everyday lives including our mental well-being. It is the hotline to Allah (SWT). Anas (RA) reported: RasulAllah (SAWS) said,

"The supplication is the essence of worship." [Sunan At-Tirmidhi]

There is a Dua about mental well-being. Abu Umamah (RA) narrates, RasulAllah (SAWS) said:

"O Allah! I seek refuge with You from worry and grief, from incapacity and laziness, from cowardice and miserliness, from being

heavily in debt and from being overpowered by (other) men." [Sahih Al-Bukhari]

Being with the Quran and making Dua is wonderful, but that is just the beginning. We as a community must play our part, we cannot just have TawakkalAllah, and say that is enough. Anas (RA) reported: A man said,

"O Messenger of Allah! Shall I tie it (camel) and rely (upon Allah), or leave it loose and rely (upon Allah)?" He said: "Tie it and rely (upon Allah)." [Sunan At-Tirmidhi]

We as a community must do our part by removing the stigma that mental issues do not exist. The Masajid must lead this effort by having khutbahs and lectures to reinforce the notion that having mental health issues is normal and is not a sign of weak faith. The Masajid must be places where people with mental health issues, including young adults, are comfortable in seeking assistance. It should be like a home away from home.

Every community needs to have local, accessible leaders, who have experience in the mental health field. Fortunately, many Muslims are already trained. We need to have them train imams and Masajid leadership trained to detect problems in the community. These trained professionals can also provide mental health services in health clinics, many Masajid are already running or starting mobile clinics. In addition, Masajid can have workshops run by professionals that teach the community about mental health issues and how to address them. There could be smaller breakout sessions in these workshops, where people are encouraged to discuss mental health issues.

While we wait for the capacity of Masajid to be built out these mental health functions, there are institutes like SEEMA, and the Khalil

Center. Institutes such as these fill in when there is a lack of local services. They offer virtual support sessions, educate Muslims, and try to eradicate the stigma associated with mental health issues. In 2017 the Khalil Center launched a hotline that provides a "safe and empathic space" for those in crisis situations. It is important to grow these national services to complement locally available services.

In conclusion, mental health issues are just as prevalent as physical health issues, but harder to detect. When faced with mental health issues, we must rely on the Quran and make Dua to Allah (SWT) to alleviate them. As a community, we must address this crisis in the Ummah. The Masajid must work to remove the stigma that mental problems do not exist or reflect weak Iman. Masajid must also improve access to professional mental health services by partnering with locally trained professionals. We should also promote and grow nationally available services to help those with mental health problems. I would like to end with the beautiful words of Ibn Al-Qayyim regarding mental health:

"A friend will not (literally) share your struggles, and a loved one cannot physically take away your pain, and a close one will not stay up the night on your behalf. So, look after yourself, protect yourself, nurture yourself, and do not give life's events more than what they are really worth."

3rd Place: Khairun Nessa
National Ideal Girls' College, Dhaka

There are indeed many challenges that high schoolers face daily in their teenager lives. These challenges are mental, physical, emotional, social, etc. These problems not only destroy teenagers mentally, physically but morally also. They can destroy teenagers' innocence too. So, to avoid these challenges and stay positive and mentally healthy there are many ways in Islam. As a Muslim by following the paths which Quran and Hadith show, teenagers can have a sound mind. Even getting advice from elders, social awareness, and community support can make teenagers stress-free.

The teenage years are also called adolescence. This is a time for growth spurts and puberty changes (sexual maturation). A teen faces many changes in her/his life. Here's a look at the changes for boys and girls:

1. **Physical changes:** Physical changes happen due to change in the teenager's hormone levels.
   - The development of full breasts in girls can be awkward in the beginning. Girls start to feel conscious about their figure.
   - Change of the voice and the appearance of facial hair in boys is perhaps the most prominent change that takes place during adolescence.

2. **Emotional changes and problems:** Hormones affect teenagers not only physically but also emotionally.
   - Teenagers are often confused about their role and as they are torn between their responsibilities as growing adults and their desires as children.
   - They tend to feel overly emotional. Just about anything and everything can make them happy, excited, mad, or angry.

- Mood swings are common among teenagers because of hormonal changes.
- Bodily changes result in self-consciousness.

3. **Psychological problems:** Research has revealed that around 50% of teenagers face mental health disorders at the age of 14. At that time, one-third of adolescent suicidal deaths occur by depression. The most common mental health disorders observed during adolescence are anxiety and mood disorders. Social phobias and panic disorders are common among this age group. Girls may tend to have more vulnerability to develop depressive disorders than boys.
   - Depression is one of the common psychological problems associated with adolescence.
   - Eating disorders are also psychosomatic as they start with the adolescent having a poor self- image and the need to change the way they look by any means.

4. **Social problems:** Attraction to the opposite sex begins during puberty. Adolescence is the time when their sexual or reproductive organs start developing.
   - Teenagers need time to understand and get comfortable with their sexuality. Girls and boys start experiencing 'weird' feelings towards the other sex and may not know what to do about it.
   - Competition is another important aspect of a teenager's social life.

Teenagers go through many mental and physical changes which demotivate them in their life very badly. But to stay positive and mentally healthy Islamic knowledge can help them. As we know Islam values the importance of good mental health and emotional wellbeing. The Qur'an can be used as a guide to those suffering from emotional distress and aims to lead people to a meaningful quality of life.

"There is no disease that Allah has created, except that He also has created its treatment" [Sahih Al-Bukhari]

As a Muslim, people get affected by life's troubles and disturbing thoughts like everyone else, but they can deal with them much better because they have a clear roadmap of where they came from, where they are going and why, so they have a head start having this fundamental knowledge from its source. Someone who feels completely lost and alone in the face of a crisis would probably feel helpless and depressed. In Holy Quran Allah (SWT) has mentioned,

"And we send down, of the Quran, that which is a healing and a mercy to the believers." [Al-Quran; 17:82]

But someone who feels supported by a compassionate God who genuinely cares, who listens to desperate pleas, and who grants generous help, has a better chance of getting back on track much faster because there is a strong helping hand to reach for while dealing with life's trouble.

"And whoever fears Allah - He will make for him a way out; And will provide for him from where he does not expect. And whoever relies upon Allah - then He is sufficient for him. Indeed, Allah will accomplish His purpose. Allah has already set for everything a [decreed] extent." [Al-Quran; 65:2-3]

On the other hand, adults in our lives and our community can help young people like us in many ways. They are-

- Friendly behavior between young and old people in society.
- Adults should understand the feelings of teenagers.
- Parents should be more conscious about their children's behavior and emotions.

- Parents should be friendly with their children.
- The adult should give religious knowledge to the youngsters.
- The community or society where children are living should arrange moral and motivational programs to encourage teenagers to do good things in their life.
- Social awareness about wrong and right things can play a great role.
- Religious programs like competitions, Islamic concerts can help teenagers to avoid committing sins.

In conclusion, it is common to face changes, challenges in the teenage years. But Muslims should remember Allah in times of suffering and pain and have faith and hope in his mercy and compassion to ease the suffering. As Allah says in Quran,

"And when you have decided, then rely upon Allah. Indeed, Allah loves those who rely [upon Him]." [Al-Quran; 3:159]

APPENDIX A

From the EPC Community

Participants in the Essay Panel Contest have shared their experiences and, in several instances, made efforts to give back to the endeavor by volunteering their own time and areas of expertise. Here are some of their comments.

"I still remember the feeling of butterflies in my stomach before it was my turn to present my speech. There were years when I didn't want to participate because, for me, writing was always a struggle. But when it came time to speak, there was always this rush of excitement. To this day, I still get butterflies in my stomach before a big presentation, but all the practice I got from EPC and this platform, in general, has helped me build my confidence in public speaking, alhamdulillah. I have been a part of EPC for over 12-13 years as a competitor and now a judge. I love hearing the new voices of our next generation, and seeing the great skills, the Muslim youth have to offer Ma shaa Allah."

- **Danya Chowdhury, EPC Judge & Past Participant**

"It is important that the leaders of tomorrow be able to communicate effectively and confidently, especially in front of large audiences. Starting at a young age gives our children time for growth and positive feedback. The EPC is a fun and encouraging way to develop these skills and will undoubtedly help them in the future. Thank you for all that you do!"

- **Hayder and Humaira Qaadri, EPC Parents**

APPENDIX B

Submission Guidelines

DO NOT write your name or any personal information on the body of the text. Use Times New Roman, 12-point font; no image is allowed in the text. Submit simple text only.

You must register. Your registration information must include your name, address, phone number, grade level, the school/College you are attending, and the organization (Islamic Center) you represent.

Online submission (MS WORD Format) is **required.**

- DO **NOT use multiple entries for the same submission. One essay per submission.**
- **On the subject line, mention:** EPC 2022, your level, your grade, your last name and first initial, your institution, and the name of the topics (see "sample: essay submission email")
- **Attach a word document following the directions given above.**
- **Scanned submission of the letter for Level I only.** Please submit your scanned letter using the JotForm provided. Your letter should not exceed three pages. DO NOT write your name or personal information on the letter. Follow the registration information.

Appendix B

- References must be cited using the APA Format (http://owl.english.purdue.edu/owl/resource/560/01/) - for Quran citation use (Sura#: Ayah#), and for Hadith, use (Source, Hadith #) or APA format
- Written statements from the parent/guardian and the author confirming that the work was primarily done by the author (Book publication requires that the work is original and their own.)
- EPC contest is a 3-phase event: Writing, speaking, and publishing.
- Top contestants in the Written Essay contest of each level will participate in the Speech Contest. Therefore, preparing and rephrasing the essay for the speech is highly encouraged for all participants upon completing their essays.
- Preregistration is required for participation in the annual EPC contest.
- All essays, posters, and multimedia submitted for this contest become the property of the Mafiq Foundation. The Mafiq Foundation reserves the exclusive right to use these materials for publishing, circulating, and promotional purposes.
- An honor statement stating the type of help and the level of effort that you received from your parents, teachers, or others in preparing the essay must be included. A sample honor statement is shown below.

EPC HONOR STATEMENT

I understand that i**t is a violation of the Academic integrity to use unauthorized materials or work from others without proper citation.** I promise that I did not copy, nor someone else write down the essay for me. I further promise that the essay was researched, organized, and written by me with no help or limited help from my parents or others, and that the work presented herein is entirely my own.

Name of Participant | Date | Name of Parent

APPENDIX C

List of all participants for 2020, 2021, and 2022

Participant Name	School Name	City and State
	Level 1	
Abyaz Ibne Akter	Park International School & College	Dhaka, Bangladesh
Ali Cheema	Washington International Academy	Alexandria, VA
Alisha Memon	Al Fatih School	Reston, VA
Amin Cheema	Washington International Academy	Alexandria, VA
Amira Ahmed Minsa	Park International School & College	Dhaka, Bangladesh
Anan Ibnul Hasan	Park International School & College	Dhaka, Bangladesh
Arisha Habib	Park International School & College	Dhaka, Bangladesh
Bilal G	Homeschool	Lanham, MD
Dua Syed	ADAMS Center	Sterling, VA
Hamza Rajper	Tarbiyah Academy	Elkridge, MD
Iyaad Minhaz	Park International School & College	Dhaka, Bangladesh

Jenna Armouche	Washington International Academy	Alexandria, VA
Mahathir Faruque	Park International School & College	Dhaka, Bangladesh
Mahim-ul Chowdhury	OTHER	Reston, VA
Maryam Karim	OTHER	Lanham, MD
Md. Akbor Hossain	Park International School & College	Dhaka, Bangladesh
Md. Wasil Hossain Riyasat	Park International School & College	Dhaka, Bangladesh
Merium Ahmad	OTHER	Lanham, MD
Mian Harris Kamal	Al Rahmah School	Baltimore, MD
Mohibuzzaman Safwan	Park International School and College	Dhaka, Bangladesh
Noora Khan	Al Fatih School	Reston, VA
Qasim Monib	ICCL	Laurel, MD
Rafia Khanam Raha	Park International School & College	Dhaka, Bangladesh
Raidah Islam	Al Huda School	College Park, MD
Ridima Alam	Park International School & College	Dhaka, Bangladesh
Safwan Choudhury	Greenbelt Elementary	Greenbelt, MD
Saim Hasan	Washington International Academy	Alexandria, VA
Samah Choudhury	OTHER	Greenbelt, MD

Appendix C

Sharik al Hasan	Park International School & College	Dhaka, Bangladesh
Tariq Uddin	Washington International Academy	Alexandria, VA
Tasfia Amin	Park International School & College	Dhaka, Bangladesh
Tashin Mahmud Ayan	Park International School & College	Dhaka, Bangladesh
Uthman Ali	Homeschooling	Lanham, MD
Yaaseen Ahmed	ICCL	Laurel, MD
Yousuf Syed	ADAMS Center	Sterling, VA
Yusuf Munir	Tarbiyah Academy	Elkridge, MD
Zainab Abdul Basit	Tarbiyah Academy	Elkridge, MD
Zaynab Mehmood	MCC	Silver Spring, MD
Zaynab Mehmood	OTHER	Howard County, MD
Aasiyah Rajper	Tarbiyah Academy	Laurel, MD
Abdullah Maher	Park International School & College	Dhaka, Bangladesh
Abdullah Syed	ADAMS Center	Sterling, VA
Airo Keri	Al Huda School	College Park, MD
Alesha Khan	Al Huda School	College Park, MD
Alina Maheen	OTHER	Ellicott City, MD
Amena Noor	Park International School & College	Dhaka, Bangladesh

Arwa Suliman	Al-Rahmah School	Baltimore, MD
Ayaan Qureshi	OTHER	Ellicott City, MD
Cali Ali	OTHER	Lanham, MD
Eliza Khan	OTHER	Virginia
Fareedah Imran	Al-Rahmah School	Maryland
Fatima Abdalla	Al-Rahmah School	Baltimore, MD
Hamza-Syed Ali	OTHER	Gaithersburg, MD
Hannah Mirza	Al-Rahmah School	Catonsville, MD
Hazera Choudhury	Al-Rahmah School	Baltimore, MD
Humayun Dahya	Tarbiyah Academy	Elkridge, MD
Idris Miller	Al Rahmah School	Baltimore, MD
Liyana Monir	OTHER	Baltimore, MD
Mahajabin Afroz Mehek	Park International School & College	Dhaka, Bangladesh
Mariam Ali	Homeschool	Champaign, IL
Merium Ahmad	OTHER	Lanham, MD
Mian Harris Kamal	Al-Rahmah School	Baltimore, MD
Musa Rahmani	Washington International Academy	Alexandria, VA
Musa Rahmani	OTHER	Falls Church, VA
Mustafaa Ahmed	M&M Learning Center	College Park, MD
Nabeeha Nur	Park International School & College	Dhaka, Bangladesh

Appendix C

Raihan Ahmed	OTHER	Bridgewater, VA
Raima Noor	Park International School & College	Dhaka, Bangladesh
Raniya Miller	Al-Rahmah School	Baltimore, MD
Rijja Mughal	Tarbiyah Academy	Elkridge, MD
Rumaisha Azwa	Park International School & College	Dhaka, Bangladesh
Saad Mahfuz	PGMA- Diyanet Center of America	Lanham, MD
Safwan Choudhury	OTHER	Green Belt, MD
Sakeena Maniar	Al-Rahmah School	Baltimore, MD
Sanari Khermiche	M&M Learning Center	College Park, MD
Shahariya Boni	Park International School & College	Dhaka, Bangladesh
Suhaan Talukder	Al-Rahmah school	Baltimore, MD
Sulaiman Mansuri	Homeschool	Chicago, IL
Sumayyah Ahmad	OTHER	Herndon, VA
Sumayyah Islam	Diyanet Center of America	Lanham, MD
Suraia Sirat	Park International School & College	Dhaka, Bangladesh
Syeda Naffatul Jinan	Park International School & College	Dhaka, Bangladesh
Ubaida Binte Khan Nusaiba	Park International School & College	Dhaka, Bangladesh
Uthman Ali	Homeschooling	Lanham, MD

Yaaseen Ahmed	ICCL	Laurel, MD
Yerfana Jannat	Park International School & College	Dhaka, Bangladesh
Yousuf Ali	Al-Rahmah School	Baltimore, MD
Yusuf Mehmood	MCC	Baltimore, MD
Zahara Khermiche	M&M Learning Center	College Park, MD
Zakariya Qaaddri	OTHER	Lanham, MD
Zaynab Salman	Washington International Academy	Alexandria, VA

Level 3

Abubeker Kemal	Al Huda School	College Park MD
Adam Khan	ADAMS Center	Herndon, VA
Aisha Ahmed	King Abdullah Academy	Herndon, VA
Ammaar Syed	OTHER	Herndon, VA
Ashaj Hossain	ADAMS Center	Sterling, VA
Cali Ali	Homeschooling	Lanham, MD
Dawud Mansuri	OTHER USA school	Champaign, IL
Dawud Qaadri	OTHER	Lanham, MD
Fatimah Karim	Homeschooling	Lanham, MD
Hafsah Khan	Clarksville Elementary School	Clarksville, MD
Hakeem Ahmed	Al-Minar Academy	Herndon, VA
Hamza-Syed Ali	Home Schooling	Gaithersburg, MD

Appendix C

Idris Miller	Al Rahmah School	Baltimore, MD
Insha M	OTHER	Reston, VA
Laaibah Siddique	Al-Rahmah School	Baltimore, MD
Maria Mubasshira	Park International School & College	Dhaka, Bangladesh
Mariyah Mehmood	MCC	Baltimore, MD
Mariyam Paracha	OTHER	Sterling, VA
Maryam Syed	OTHER	Herndon, VA
Mikdad Jawad	Other- NON-USA school	Dhaka, Bangladesh
Musa Rahmani	Al-Fatih Academy	Reston, VA
Mustafaa Ahmed	M&M Learning Center	Lanham, MD
Nubaid Shaik	OTHER	Herndon, VA
Nurah Cheema	Washington International Academy	Alexandria, VA
Rafsan Rayhan	Park International School & College	Dhaka, Bangladesh
Rahmah Mohamed	OTHER	Sterling, VA
Raif Bhuyan	Tarbiyah Academy	Elkridge, MD
Rania Ahmed	OTHER	Bridgewater, VA
Ruwayda Mursalin Amin	Park International School & College	Dhaka, Bangladesh
Saadiq Ahmed	M&M Learning Center	College Park, MD
Sakeena Mansuri	OTHER	Champaign, IL
Samera Ali	OTHER	Lanham, MD

Sarah Hussen	Washington International Academy	Alexandria, VA
Sarah Sawadogo	Homeschooling	Champaign, IL
Sarina Sheikh	OTHER	Sterling, VA
Shabbir Khan	OTHER	Ellicott City, MD
Shaza Elsayed	Washington International Academy	Alexandria, VA
Sophia Ahmed	OTHER	Bridgewater, VA
Subata Binte Nasir	Park International School & College	Dhaka, Bangladesh
Sumayyah Islam	OTHER	Silver Spring, VA
Tasneem Elzend	Washington International Academy	Alexandria, VA
Tasneem-Syeda Ali	OTHER	Gaithersburg, MD
Tohaiya Chowdhury	Park International School & College	Dhaka, Bangladesh
Yara Hijab	Home Schooling	Urbana, IL
Yaseen Dardir	Homeschooling	Urbana, IL
Yusuf Mehmood	MCC	Silver Spring, MD
Yusuf Mehmood	Homeschooling	Howard County MD
Zakariya Faisal	OTHER	Silver Spring, VA
Zakariya Qaadri	OTHER	Lanham, MD
Zuhaer Ashab	Park International School & College	Dhaka, Bangladesh

Appendix C

Level 4

AbdurRahman Ahmad	OTHER	Herndon, VA
Adil Salih	Al-Huda School	College Park, MD
Adyan Khan	Al-Huda School	College Park, MD
Ahnaf Hossain	ADAMS Center	Sterling, VA
Alia Albasha	Al-Huda School	College Park, MD
Amber Khatib	Al-Huda School	College Park, MD
Aminnah Sayyad	Al-Huda School	College Park, MD
Areeba Rehman	Al-Huda School	College Park, MD
Arrshath Mohaideen	OTHER	Ellicott City, MD
Asiya Debencho	Al-Huda School	College Park, MD
Asma Abbas	Washington International Academy	Alexandria, VA
Asma Salhan	Al-Huda School	College Park, MD
Bilaal Rabani	Hidaya Academy	Sterling, VA
Buruj Ansari	Al-Huda School	College Park, MD
Dawud Qaadri	OTHER	Lanham, MD
Deelan Doski	Al-Huda School	College Park, MD
Fahim-ul Chowdhury	OTHER	Reston, VA
Fatma Elsayed	Washington International Academy	Alexandria, VA
Habib Basir	OTHER	Reston, VA

Hadiel Ashkar	Al-Huda School	College Park, MD
Hafsah Khan	OTHER USA school	Clarksville, MD
Hamid Diallo	Al-Huda School	College Park, MD
Hawazen Mohamed	Washington International Academy	Alexandria, VA
Heela Keri	Al-Huda School	College Park, MD
Hibah Mehreen	OTHER	Ellicott City, MD
Hidaya Isa	Al-Huda School	College Park, MD
Huda Javaid	Al-Huda school	College Park, MD
Iffat Chowdhury	Al Huda School	College Park, MD
Ikram Yosuf	Al-Huda School	College Park, MD
Iman Neja	Al-Huda School	College Park, MD
Ismael Ahmed	OTHER	McLean, VA
Jannatul Naima Rayna	Park International School & College	Dhaka, Bangladesh
Jenna Ashkar	Al-Huda School	College Park, MD
Jenna Awadallah	Al-Rahmah School	Baltimore, MD
Laiba Monir	OTHER	Baltimore, MD
Mahjujah Nawar Raita	Other Non-USA school	Dhaka, Bangladesh
Mahveen Mustafa	Al-Huda School	College Park, MD
Maisha Alam	OTHER	Herndon, VA
Mariyah Mehmood	Homeschooling	Howard County, MD
Mohamed Ahmed	Al-Huda School	College Park, MD

Appendix C

Mohsina Rahman Labonno	Park International School & College	Dhaka, Bangladesh
Nabiel Ashkar	Al-Huda School	College Park, MD
Nashmia Jaharan	ADAMS Center	Sterling, VA
Nishat Asefa	Al-Huda School	College Park, MD
Nura Hussen	Al-Huda School	College Park, MD
Nuruddin Ahamed	Al-Huda School	College Park, MD
Raisa Noor Akhi	Park International School & College	Dhaka, Bangladesh
Raqeebah Osany-inpeju	Al-Huda School	College Park, MD
Rawdatul Jannat Arshi	Park International School & College	Dhaka, Bangladesh
Rayyan Abrahim	Al-Huda School	College Park, MD
Razan Masri	Al-Huda School	College Park, MD
Ruqayya Khan	Al-Huda School	College Park, MD
Ruwad Islam	Al-Huda School	College Park, MD
Saadiq Ahmed	OTHER	Beltsville, MD
Sabirah Burt	Al-Huda School	College Park, MD
Sakinah Ozair	OTHER -USA school	College Park, MD
Samera Ali	Homeschooling	Lanham, MD
Sara Kamili	Al-Huda school	College Park, MD
Sara Khan	Al-Huda School	College Park, MD
Sarah Mohamed	Al-Minar School	Herdon, VA

Sarina Neja	Al-Huda School	College Park, MD
Setra Said	Al-Huda School	College Park, MD
Shehbaz Khan	OTHER	Maryland
Sidrah Shalabi	Al-Huda School	College Park, MD
Soondus Rashed	Al-Huda School	College Park, MD
Sumaya Adan	Al-Huda School	College Park, MD
Taha Siddiqi	OTHER	Sterling, VA
Tasneem-Syeda Ali	OTHER	Gaithersburg, MD
Tasnem Ahmad	Tarbiyah Academy	Elkridge, MD
Yousef Abdeldayem	M&M Learning Center	Lanham, MD
Zaina Issa	Homeschooling	Urbana, IL
Zanib Shamrez	Al-Huda School	College Park, MD
Zina Brahimi	Al-Huda School	College Park, MD

Level 5

Abid Noor	Al-Huda School	College Park, MD
Bushra Larijani	OTHER	Reston, VA
Ebadutt Malik	Al-Huda School	College Park, MD
Emira- Syeda Ali	OTHER	Gaithersburg, MD
Hadiya Zayed	Al-Huda School	College Park, MD
Hafiza Chowdhury	OTHER	Herndon, VA
Haniya Salih	Al-Huda School	College Park, MD
Hawa Mohamed	Al-Huda School	College Park, MD
Hayat Sultan	Al-Huda School	College Park, MD
Kabineh Kakay	Al-Huda School	College Park, MD
Khadijah Samiya	OTHER	Greenbelt, MD

Appendix C

Mabinty Savage	Al-Huda School	College Park, MD
Mian Haroon Kamal	OTHER	Baltimore, MD
Muhammad Islam	OTHER	Fulton, MD
Musa Ahmad	OTHER	Lanham, MD
Nabeel Chowdhury	Al-Huda School	College Park, MD
Nuruddin Ahamed	Al-Huda School	Reston, VA
Omar Ali	OTHER	Lanham, MD
Salihah Burt	Al-Huda School	College Park, MD
Sulayman Khan	OTHER	Greenbelt, MD
Sumeya Kemal	Al-Huda School	College Park, MD
Syed Hossain	OTHER	Virginia
Zahra Shamrez	Al-Huda School	College Park, MD

Level 6

Emira-Syeda Ali	Homeschooling	Gaithersburg, MD
Jannah Nassar	OTHER	Clarksville, MD
Khadija Bah	Al-Huda School	College Park, MD
Khairun nessa	National Ideal Girls College	Dhaka, Bangladesh
Omar Ali	OTHER	Lanham, MD
Raakin Kabir	ADAMS Center	Sterling, VA

APPENDIX D

EPC Judges- Past and Present

Abdul Mukheeth is a scientist and has judged EPC in the past.

Abu Syed Mahfuz is an author and published 5 books, including forthcoming book on Software Quality, Information Security and Audit, to be published by International Publisher Taylor & Francis Group. An Information Technology Professional at Hewlett Packard Enterprise, he has a Masters' degree in Software Management from University of Detroit Mercy, Michigan and another Masters in Shariah Law from International Islamic University Malaysia. He has been the editor and publisher of Bangla Amar Newspaper for over 10 years.

Afaaf Amir Ahmad is a former EPC participant and a graduate in Islamic Jurisprudence from the International Islamic University of Malaysia.

Ameenah Cowels is currently an English teacher at Al-Huda School, College Park, MD. She has been teaching at Al-Huda for the past three years. She has four daughters and one cat. Ameenah received her BA from Rowan University in English and Secondary Education. Prior to getting her degree, Ameenah spent 20 years in the United States Air Force as a Public Health Technician, and she provided public health, communicable disease and food handling education. During her tour in England, Ameenah and her family reverted to Islam.

Appendix D

Amirah Ahmad is a former EPC participant and a Master of Public Policy student at the University of Maryland. She received a B.A. in Islamic Jurisprudence from the International Islamic University of Malaysia and hopes to help and encourage Muslim youth in developing skills to become community leaders, thinkers, and reformers.

Amreen Ahmed has recently relocated to Maryland. She believes this is an opportunity for her to get involved in her new community, and she hopes to be able to contribute in the future, insha Allah.

Anum Shami resides in Maryland. She is a mom of 3, and a clinical pharmacist at University of Maryland Medical Center. She is also the founder of Muslim Scouts of Maryland. The group aims to give back to the community through service activities and creates a safe and creative place for the young kids.

Arif Kabir is a Product Manager at Deloitte Digital and is pursuing his Masters' degree in Human Computer Interaction at the University of Maryland. He has completed his Hifdh and studies Islamic sciences at AlMaghrib Institute with his family. He is the Editor-in-Chief of Muslim Youth Musings, an online literary magazine for youth. He has a passion for spreading literature and therefore would love to spread the work of EPC.

Asim Ghafoor has over two decades of experience in advising public policymakers and clients on a variety of legal, political, and trade issues. He is a frequent speaker at seminars, conferences, and in the media on topics of law enforcement, international affairs, finance and politics. He has spoken at Harvard, the University of Virginia School of Law, and Chicago's Kent College of Law. Previously, Mr. Ghafoor worked in the Texas House of Representatives, giving him great insight into the legislative and law-making process. From 1997 – 2000, Asim Ghafoor served as Legislative Assistant to Congressman Ciro D. Rodriguez (D-TX) and advised the Congressman on a variety of issues, including international affairs, banking, civil rights, transportation, armed services and veterans' affairs. Mr. Ghafoor earned his JD from the University of Texas School of Law. He is married and has three children.

Doha Nassar is a 2nd grade teacher in Montgomery County. She graduated from the University of Maryland with a bachelor's degree in Elementary Education and a minor in Human Development. When she is not in the classroom, she enjoys spending time with family, going out in nature, and trying new recipes in the kitchen. She started competing in EPC when she was in third grade and found the competition helped improve her writing and speech skills.

Gibran Ali is a Software Engineer by profession who graduated from the University of Maryland, College Park, in December '12, majoring in Computer Science. He is also the program coordinator at the Youth Group at the Prince George's Muslim Association. He believes the EPC is a very powerful platform through which the youth can express themselves and learn the skills required to become leaders in the community.

Hasannah Ali is currently teaching 1st grade at Al-Huda School. She has a degree in Psychology and is pursuing a higher degree in Educational Psychology at UMBC. Having attended Al-Huda and a local homeschooling program, she has participated in the EPC several times and has also been a part of many panel discussions.

Hasan Ahmed is a scientist and attorney by training.

Hena Zuberi is the Editor in Chief of Muslimmatters.org, an award-winning web magazine. A community organizer for years, she resides in the Washington DC metro, with her husband and four children, where she is the staff reporter for the Muslim Link newspaper. Hena transitioned from television into print and social journalism after working as a TV news reporter and producer for CNBC Asia and World Television News (now Associated Press TV). Most recently, Hena's work has been published in the Tree of Life - a resource book by CHAI Parenting Initiative, a nonprofit dedicated to mental health and wellness in the South Asian community. She was featured on American Public Media's radio show, The Story, and has spoken at the Society of Professional Journalists Conference. Hena served as the Youth Director at the Unity Center in Southern California for ten years. She uses her experience with youth to conduct Growing Up with God workshops in communities around the country.

Imam Ali Siddiqui teaches Islam, comparative religion, History of Islam and Muslims of Americas, contemporary issues to Muslims and non-Muslims at the institutions of higher learning as a Visiting Faculty member at various institutions. Some of these institutions are Sonoma State, Santa Rosa Community College, School of Religion (Claremont Graduate University), California Baptist University, Disciple of Christ Seminary, School of Theology (now Lincoln University), and La Verne University, and Open University Denver. He has been on many successful speaking tours to Belgium, Canada, Germany, Great Britain, Iran, Pakistan, Spain, Switzerland, and across the USA.

Jawaad Khan is a writer and filmmaker out of South Florida, and currently serves as a Literary Editor for the online literary magazine Muslim Youth Musings.

Kamran Anwar is a biological scientist working in the biotechnology industry. After obtaining his PhD from SUNY Downstate Medical Center, he and his family moved to Maryland for post-doctoral fellowship at the NIH. He currently resides in the DC suburbs of Maryland.

Kashif M Munir is an Assistant Professor in the Division of Endocrinology at the University of Maryland School of Medicine. He currently sits on the boards of the Financial Independence Group of America, Al-Madina Foundation, and Dar al Islam. He also volunteers for WhyIslam (DC Chapter), and reviews books for Fons Vitae publishing. He has been actively involved in various capacities with the EPC and Muslim Youth debate platforms for several years. He currently lives in Howard County with his wife and children.

Kimberly Baqqi graduated in Biology from Morgan State University and attended Drexel Medical College for post-graduate studies. She is actively involved within the community, including leading a Girl Scout Troop for Muslim girls for the past three years. Her focus, however, is on homeschooling her three beautiful children and she is most passionate about children and education. She participated three years in a row as a judge for MIST and thoroughly enjoyed the process. She is grateful for the opportunity to positively influence, encourage, and empower our youth, both for MIST and EPC in any way she can.

Kulsoom Khan is a former public high-school & middle-school Social Studies teacher in both Baltimore County and DuPage County (Illinois). She is an advocate for the written word. She believes that writing is a personal journey in which an individual thinks deeply, organizes, and express ideas in a thoughtful and powerful manner. She appreciates when young adults put forth extra thought and effort to produce a quality piece of work for forums like the EPC. As an American Muslim, she sees rhetoric as a powerful tool in helping promote understanding & respect amongst all walks of life in our country and abroad.

Mahfuz Rahman has been coaching/mentoring local youths in essay writing, reviewing and providing feedback on essays. He believes that EPC is a great platform that can significantly contribute

Appendix D

to the development of writing skills for our youth. He has previously judged essays in EPC competitions.

Maryam Ahmad has participated in MYDT as a participant for 5 years and worked with them closely. She has been a judge at the MYDT and has also acted as a Judge's Coordinator. She is a Junior at Zaytuna College, a Liberal Arts College.

Maryam Ishaq is a recent graduate from the University of Maryland with a Bachelors in Biochemistry. She is currently in the process of applying for graduate school in pursuit of working in the healthcare field.

Mecca Mustafa works as a journalist for the Muslim link. She recently graduated from UMD with a degree in English and minors in creative writing and Arabic, and she participated in the EPC competition when she was a student at Al-Rahmah school.

Meryam is a student at UMUC majoring in English. She had never judged in a competition before, so this has been a new and very enjoyable experience for her.

Misba Samiya is a student at University of Maryland College Park. She has judged multimedia/poster sessions in the past.

Musfika Hossain is currently an English teacher at Al-Huda School, College Park, MD. She earned her Master's in Education in Secondary English from the University of Maryland. She has been involved in the Dar-us-Salaam community as a volunteer and teacher of Quranic studies for many years.

Nadia Hasan has an MBA degree, is a social entrepreneur, business planning strategist, government relations professional, specialist in non- profit and human resource management, a public speaker, a youth trainer and educator, media contributor, social justice advocate, daughter of US Marine, and a California girl from Orange County. She is the founder and director of Young Leaders Institute, a youth leadership platform and network connector that empowers youth toward social entrepreneurship.

Nazea Khan is a senior at the University of Maryland, College Park. She was born and raised in Silver Spring, Maryland.

Nishath Fatima is a college student who offered her time to judge the competition in order to help EPC grow and to encourage more and more people to enjoy EPC and learn more about Islam.

Nishwath Samiya is currently a student at University of Maryland, College Park. She has been a part of EPC since middle school and believes it is an excellent platform for Muslim youth.

Rehenuma Asmi is an Assistant Professor at Allegheny College in the Department of Philosophy and Religious Studies. She is also affiliated with the Education and International Studies Programs. She believes that the essay competition allows her to give back to the Muslim community and to learn about the issues of interest to Muslim youth today.

Ruqayyah Khan is currently pursuing an undergraduate degree at George Washington University.

Shadia Nahar is a Biochemistry and Molecular Biology student at UMBC. She participated in various Mafiq competitions like EPC and MYDT and recently judged their annual debate competition. She is also a published author with works that primarily focus on the stigma surrounding American Muslims and hopes that young Muslims are influenced by these various programs as she was when she was younger.

Appendix D

Safiyyah Fatima has been working with youth in the education sector since she was 12. Tutoring, and conducting online reading outreach programs for local non-profit organizations is her specialty. She is also passionate about writing and is working on publishing a WWII veteran's memoir at 19 years of age.

Saira Sufi has over 10 years of professional experience in the event management field. She holds a B.A. in Political Science from the University of Kansas and has her Event Management Certificate from George Washington University and is currently pursuing her Certified Meeting Planner designation. She has an extensive background in political, nonprofit and government event coordination. Prior to joining Booz Allen Hamilton, Ms. Sufi worked for the Presidential Inauguration Committee as well as the Obama Presidential Campaign. Before joining the campaign, Ms. Sufi worked as the Director of Events for the Center for Social Leadership, focusing on improving the operations of non-profit organizations. Saira offered her time to judge EPC submissions because she feels it is important for Muslim youth to grow spiritually through educational forums. She hopes this will be a learning experience for all involved, particularly regarding how the Muslim Ummah can be strengthened.

Sakinah Ishaq is a Public Health graduate from the University of Maryland, and she is currently working at a doctor's office as a healthcare administrator. She is currently in the pursuit of furthering her education through graduate school.

Prof. M. Saleet Jafri is currently Professor and Chair of the Department of Bioinformatics and Computational Biology at George Mason University. He has published over 40 peer reviewed journal articles. He holds affiliate appointments at the Center for Biomedical Engineering and Technology at the University of Maryland Baltimore. He received his BS in mathematics from Duke University, a MS in mathematics from the Courant Institute of Mathematical Science at New York University, and a PhD in Biomathematical Sciences from the Mount Sinai School of Medicine/City University of New York.

Sarah Arafat is a senior at Notre Dame of Maryland University majoring in biology to pursue a career in dentistry. She participated in EPC as a contestant for nine consecutive years and plans to stay involved with EPC for years to come inshaAllah. In addition to being a full- time student, she is the president of her university's Muslim Student Association and Biology Honor Society and serves as a private Qur'an tutor for children in the Baltimore area. She values diversity, cultural competency, the concept of global citizenship and believes we can all contribute to improving society today.

Sophia Sirage currently works at a tech company, and is the founder of Al-Arkaan, a nonprofit dedicated to making Islamic knowledge accessible. She also currently studies at Qalam Seminary, in the Alimiyyah Program.

Sumaiyah Khan works as a Literary Editor for Muslim Youth Musings. Having participated in EPC when she was younger and having fond memories associated with it, she wished to get involved with judging the competition. Her experience with EPC helped her and her friends gain invaluably from this competition, and she believes it's important and beneficial for students to practice exploring their thoughts and challenging themselves through writing.

Susan Jenkins works as a Social Science analyst with the US Department of Health and Human Services and has a PhD in Psychology from the University of Michigan. She has served as an EPC judge for almost 10 years and serves our youth as a Girls Scout leader with Troop 223 through the Islamic Society of Baltimore.

Appendix D

Tasmeea Noor started her career as an architect, and then switched to Information Technology in the mid-1990s. As time permits, she utilizes her technology background for Allah's work. During her student life in Bangladesh, she was an occasional writer for local newspapers. She enjoys active engagement that leads to spiritual growth. She lives in Maryland and is the mother of two daughters.

Tayaabah Qazi is an educator and a mother of two teenagers. After graduating from UCLA in Neuroscience, she joined the teaching profession and acquired a Teaching Certification in Chemistry and a Masters' degree in Educational Leadership. In addition to teaching, she has also played an integral role as a Vice Principal at Islamic Schools for three years and as an Educational Program Developer for a year. Currently, she is engaged in homeschooling and providing educational support to homeschooling families by various means, in the Baltimore County Area.

Wasif Sikder is a computer engineering student at UMD College Park.

Yasir Diab is a patent examiner for the USPTO. He is an avid reader and has been happy to be a part of an initiative that he believes encourages our youth to fine-tune their writing skills and expand their horizons by maintaining a consistent and persistent curious nature.

Yumna Rahman is currently a third-year Computer Science student at the University of Virginia with a concentration in Creative Writing and Women, Gender, and Sexuality. She has been a participant in EPC since she was twelve and was happy to continue contributing to EPC as a judge last year. Additionally, Mafiq and EPC hold a very dear place in her heart as she has fond memories of participating in the competition ever since the third grade. She always enjoys reading the thoughts of growing writers and speakers and has really enjoyed this opportunity.

Zahra Ahmed is a Family Practitioner practicing at DUS Family Medical Practice in Greenbelt, MD. She became a member of the EPC Committee in 2005 after her eldest daughter participated in the essay competition for the first time. She instantly appreciated such a forum for our youth to be able to express themselves through writing and speech on various topics addressing who they are as Muslims living in America. She believes that our future as Muslims in the West is becoming more and more uncertain. Therefore, she wishes to see a panel such as this get to a national level where the voices of our youth can be heard across the nation, insha Allah.

Zahra Aligabi is currently pursuing an undergraduate degree at University of Maryland.

Zaakira Ahmed is currently pursuing an undergraduate degree at University of Maryland.

Zaafira Elham is currently pursuing an undergraduate degree at University of Maryland.

APPENDIX E

Glossary of Arabic/Islamic Terminology

Throughout the book, there are several salutations used to show the utmost respect to Allah as the Creator and to and to the prophets who carried His message. For ease of reading these salutations have been abbreviated as follows:

(AS) [عليه السلام]: Alayhis-salaam/ Alayhas-salaam/ Alayhumas-salaam– Peace be upon him/her/them. This salutation is used following the name of any of the prophets.

(RA) [راضي الله عنه]: Radi-Allahu 'anhu/ Radi- Allahu 'anha/ Radi-Allahu 'anhum– May Allah be pleased with him/her/them. This salutation is used following the name of any of the Prophet Muhammad's family or immediate companions.

(SAWS/ SAW) [صلى الله عليه وسلم]: SalAllahu 'alayhi wa sallam– Peace and blessings be upon him. This salutation is used following the name of the Prophet Muhammad. Although all the prophets of Allah are highly regarded for their missions and sacrifice, the Prophet Muhammad holds a higher status as the messenger who received the words of Allah in the form of the Quran, the final and complete guidance for all of mankind.

(SWT) [سبحانة وتعالى]: Subhanahu wa ta'ala– Glory to Him, the Highest. This salutation is used following the name of Allah.

Adhan [أذان]: The call to prayer made using the human voice rather than with something like a horn or bell.

AH: After Hijrah. The Hijrah was the event of the emigration of Prophet Muhammad (SAWS) from Makkah to Madinah and signifies the beginning of the Islamic calendar.

Ajar [اجر]: Reward.

Akhirah [ألآخره]: The Hereafter.

Al-Fatihah [ألفاتحه]: The opening chapter or first surah of the Quran.

Alhamdullilah [الحمد لله]: All praise and thanks are due to Allah.

Allah [الله]: The Supreme Creator of the universe and all that exists, whom all Muslims worship. The word Allah is derived from the Arabic word 'ilah' (meaning God). The word 'Allah' has no plural or feminine. In contrast, the English word 'god' has a plural form (gods) and a feminine form (goddess). The word Allah should always be used in its place.

Arafat [عرفه]: A plain and mountain situated to the north of Makkah. Pilgrims gather here between midday and sunset on the ninth day of Dhul Hijjah (the last month of the Islamic calendar) to pray for Allah's forgiveness.

Assalaamu Alaikum [السلام عليكم]: Peace be upon you. This is the greeting one should give to his/her fellow Muslims. The reply to this is 'Wa alaikum as salaam' (And upon you be peace).

Ayah [آية] (pl: ayaat آيات): A verse from the Quran. Literally meaning sign (which leads or directs you to something important), it can also be used to describe a piece of evidence or proof.

Bismillah [بسم الله]: In the Name of Allah.

Da'wah [دعوة]: Inviting others to Islam through words or actions.

Dhikr [ذكر]: Remembrance of Allah, either through thought or speech.

Din/Deen [دين]: One's religion, faith, or way of life.

Du'a [دعاء]: Supplication or prayer to Allah (SWT).

Dunya [دنيا]: This world, or anything pertaining to it.

Eid ul-Adha [عيد الأضحى]: The Feast of Sacrifice. This Islamic holiday takes place on the 10th day of Dhul Hijjah and commemorates the Prophet Ibrahim's (AS) willingness to offer his son Ismail (AS) in sacrifice showing an act of obedience to Allah (SWT).

Eid ul-Fitr [عيد الفطر]: The Feast of Charity. This Islamic holiday marks the end of Ramadan and is observed on the 1st day of Shawwal.

Fard [فرض]: An obligatory act, such as the five daily prayers.

Fatwa [فتوى]: A legal verdict or opinion given by one or more people well-versed in Islamic law, i.e., a cleric or scholar.

Fitnah [فتنة]: Literally a test or trial but generally applies to confusion in the religion, conflicts and strife amongst people.

Fitrah [فطرة]: A person's pure state of being before it is corrupted by outside influences. This term is commonly attributed to a child at birth. Because all descendants of Adam (AS) made a covenant to Allah (SWT) when He asked, "Am I your Rabb?" Everyone answered, "Yes! We do testify." Fitrah is a natural instinct. The new reverts to Islam who have just made their shahada or declaration of faith get back to their fitrah.

Ghusl [غسل]: A full ablution/ritual bath necessary for praying after sexual intercourse or a menstrual period, for example, or the act of washing the deceased's body prior to the funeral.

Hadith [حديث]: A verified description of the words or actions of the Prophet Muhammad (SAWS).

Hajj [حج]: The fifth pillar of Islam, Hajj is the pilgrimage to Makkah which every Muslim must take once in their lifetime but only if they are healthy and able to afford it.

Halal [حلال]: Lawful or permissible according to Islamic law.

Haram [حرام]: Forbidden or prohibited according to Islamic law.

Hijab [حجاب]: A veil which covers the head, worn by Muslim women beyond the age of puberty in the presence of non-related adult males.

Hijrah [هجره]: Literally means migration and is used to describe the migration of Muslims from an enemy land to a secure place for religious causes, the first Muslims' flight from Makkah to Abyssinia (Ethiopia) and later to Madinah, and the Prophet's migration journey from Makkah to Madinah.

Hijri [هجري]: The Islamic lunar calendar, which began from the Hijrah to Madinah, is approximately 355 days and comprised of 12 months– Muharram, Safar, Rabi Al-Awwal, Rabi Al- Thani, Jumada Al- Ula, Jumada Al-Thani, Rajab, Sha'ban, Ramadan, Shawwal, Dhul Qa'adah and Dhul Hijjah.

Iblis [إبليس]: The jinn who disobeyed Allah's (SWT) order to prostrate to Adam (AS) and was expelled from His mercy (also known as Shaytan or Satan).

Imam [إمام]: The leader of any congregational prayer. It is also sometimes used to refer to the head of an Islamic state or an Islamic organization.

Iman [إيمان]: Faith, belief.

Insha'Allah [ان شاء الله]: If Allah (SWT) wills.

Islam [إسلام]: Derived from the word 'salam' (peace), Islam literally means peace through submission to Allah (SWT).

Jahannum [جهنّم]: Hellfire.

Jannah [جنّه]: Paradise.

Jannatul Firdaus [جنة الفردوس]: The highest level in Paradise.

JazakaAllahu Khairan [جزاك الله خيراً]: May Allah reward you with good.

Jibreel [جبريل]: Gabriel, the angel through whom Allah (SWT) conveyed his words to His prophets. He is also known as 'Ar Ruh al-Qudus' (The Holy Spirit).

Jihad [جهاد]: Literally means to struggle or strive and is often incorrectly interpreted as 'holy war'.

Jinn [جن]: Beings created from fire, just as angels were created from light and mankind was created from dust. Known in the Western world as spirits, demons, ghosts, etc. Like mankind, Jinn have been granted free will over their actions, therefore some are inclined to do good and some inclined to evil (unlike the angels, who are compelled by Allah (SWT) to do his bidding and therefore only do good).

Ka'bah [كعبه]: The structure in Makkah that all Muslims turn to/face while praying. It was originally built by Adam (AS), then subsequently rebuilt by Ibrahim (AS) and Ismail (AS), then finally cleansed by Prophet Muhammad (SAWS) and his followers after the pagans of Makkah had used it for their idol worship for hundreds of years.

Kafir [كافر] (pl. kuffar كفّار): A disbeliever(s) in Allah (SWT) or one who disobeys Him or joins others in worship with Him.

Khalifa [خليفه]: The leader of the Muslim nation. The most honored khulafa (leaders) were the four who ruled immediately after the death of Prophet Muhammad (SAWS): Abu Bakr, Umar, Uthman and Ali (RA).

Khutba [خطبه]: A sermon given at Jumu'ah (Friday) and Eid prayers.

Madinah [مدينه]: The holy city in present-day Saudi Arabia approximately 250 miles north of Makkah where Prophet Muhammad (SAWS) emigrated and set up the first Islamic state.

Makkah [مكّه]: The holy city in present-day Saudi Arabia in which the Ka'bah is situated and where millions of Muslims make Hajj every year.

Masjid [مسجد]: Mosque; any place for worship or prayer. The three holiest masaajid (mosques) are Al Masjid al-Haram (The Mosque of Sanctuary) located in Makkah, Al Masjid al- Nabawi (The Prophet's Mosque) located in Madinah, and Al Masjid al-Aqsa (The Furthest Mosque) located in Jerusalem.

Appendix E

Miraj [معراج]: The ascension during the "Night Journey" undertaken by Prophet Muhammad (SAWS), when he traveled to Jerusalem to the site of the Dome of the Rock (this part of the journey is called "Isra") and then he ascended to the heavens, met other prophets there, and received the command from Allah that all Muslims should pray five times a day (this part of the journey is called "Miraj").

Miskeen [مسكين]: Those who are poor.

Muslim [مسلم]: One who fully submits to the commandments of Allah (SWT).

Qiblah [قبله]: The direction facing the Ka'bah in Makkah which all Muslims face during prayer.

Qiyamah [قیامه]: Resurrection.

Quran [قرءان]: The Holy Book containing all the divine revelations as a final guidance sent to mankind through Prophet Muhammad (SAWS).

Rakah [ركعه] (pl. Rakaat ركعات): Units of prayer consisting of a series of standing, bowing, sitting and prostrating positions.

Ramadan [رمضان]: The ninth month of the Hijri calendar. It was during this month that the revelation of the Quran began, and the bloodless conquest of Makkah occurred. Muslims all over the world observe this month by fasting every day from dawn to dusk.

Rasul [رسول]: A prophet to whom Allah revealed divine texts, i.e., Musa (Moses), Dawud (David), Isa (Jesus) (AS) and Muhammad (SAWS).

Salaam [سلام]: Peace.

Salah [صلاہ] (pl. **salawat** [صلاوات]): The five obligatory prayers that Muslims must perform every day. These include Fajr (at daybreak), Dhuhr (at midday), Asr (at late afternoon), Maghrib (at sunset) and Isha (at nightfall). Additional salaat may be performed at different times throughout the day, e.g., Tahajjud, Ishraq, etc.

Sawm [صوم]: Fasting, i.e., not to eat, or drink, or have sexual relations from dawn (before adhan of Fajr prayer) till sunset. Fasting during the month of Ramadan is a pillar of faith.

Shahadah [شهادہ]: A declaration of faith, specifically "Ash-hadu an-la' ilaha illa Allahu, wa ash-hadu anna Muhammadan 'abduhu wa rasuluhu" (I testify that there are no gods besides Allah, and I testify that Muhammad is the servant and the Messenger of Allah).

Shariah [شریعہ]: Islamic law, derived from the Quran and Sunnah. The laws of Shariah are final and absolute and cannot be changed by human beings.

Shaytan [شیطان]: Satan- a devil or any jinn who is inclined to commit evil.

Shirk [شرك]: Associating, invoking, or worshiping anyone or anything besides Allah. This is the worst sin a Muslim can commit. In fact, anyone who commits this sin cannot be described as a Muslim.

SubhanAllah [سبحان الله]: Glory be to Allah.

Sunnah [سنّہ]: The sayings, practices and living habits of the Prophet Muhammad (SAWS), as recorded in the various hadith collections. Along with the Quran, the sunnah is a source of Islamic law and practice.

Appendix E

Surah/Surat [سورة]: A chapter of the Quran of which there are 114 in all.

Taqwa [تقوى]: The love and fear that a Muslim feels for Allah which drives them to avoid things that displease Him.

Tawheed [توحيد]: The declaring Allah (SWT) to be the only God. It has three aspects: Oneness of the Lordship of Allah (Tawheed ar-Rububiya), Oneness of worship of Allah (Tawheed al-Uluhiya), and Oneness of the names, qualities and the attributes of Allah (Tawheed al-Asma' was-Sifaat).

Wa Alaikum Assalam [و عليكم السلام]: And upon you be peace. This is the proper reply when someone greets you with "Assalaamu Alaikum."

Ummah [أمّة]: A single Muslim community.

Wudu [وضوء]: The ritual washing with water which must be performed before every salah.

Yateem [يتيم]: Orphan.

Zakah [زكاة]: A certain fixed proportion (2.5%) of an individual Muslim's wealth and property that is liable as zakat and paid yearly for the benefit of the poor in the Muslim community. The payment of zakah is obligatory as it is one of the five pillars of Islam. Zakah is the major economic means of establishing social and economic justice and leading the Muslim society to prosperity and security.

Zamzam [زمزم]: A sacred well inside the Masjid-al-Haram (the Grand Mosque) in Makkah.

www.ingramcontent.com/pod-product-compliance
Lightning Source LLC
Chambersburg PA
CBHW020924090426
42736CB00010B/1024